THE DESTINY SERIES

PURPOSE

BOOK 2

Rebecca D. Bennett

THE DESTINY SERIES PURPOSE ~ BOOK 2

by Rebecca D. Bennett

Copyright © 2018 by Rebecca Bennett

All rights reserved. This book is protected by the copyright laws of the United States of America. This book may not be copied or reprinted for commercial gain or profit. The use of short quotations or occasional page copying for personal or group study is encouraged. Permission will be granted upon request from Rebecca Bennett. Unless otherwise stated, all biblical quotations are taken from the New International Version. All rights reserved. Any emphasis added to scripture quotations is the author's own.

Scripture quotations marked NIV are taken from the New International Version, © 1973, 1978, 1984, 2011 by Biblica, Inc. Used by permission of Zondervan.

Scripture quotations marked AMP are taken from the Amplified Bible, © 1954, 1958, 1962, 1964, 1965, 1987 by The Lockman Foundation. Used by permission.

Scripture quotations marked MSG are taken from The Message, © 1993, 1994, 1995, 1996, 2000, 2001, 2002 by NavPress. Used by permission.

Scripture quotations marked NLT are taken from the New Living Translation, © 1996 by Tyndale House Publishers, Inc. Used by permission.

ISBN: 978-1-7370190-6-0 (paperback)

ISBN: 978-1-7370190-7-7 (e-book)

Library of Congress Control Number: 2021917305

This edition published by 3TREES PUBLISHING, LLC, Gulfport, Mississippi 39507 USA, July 2021.

Editing by Rebecca D. Bennett (rebeccadbennett.tds@gmail.com)

Layout by 3TREES PUBLISHING, LLC (3treespublishing@gmail.com)

Cover by Laura Rivera-Rexach (contact@designsxlaura.com)

CONTENTS

Copyright	ii
Introduction	v
Personal Purpose	1
1 Identifying Purpose	3
2 Purpose of Character	17
3 Purpose of Distinction	37
Ancestral Purpose...	53
4 Original Intent	55
5 Purpose of Ecclesia	69
6 Purpose of Times & Seasons	89
Kingdom Purpose	107
7 Influential Purpose	109
8 Redemptive Purpose	129
9 Purpose within Purpose	149
About the Author	163

INTRODUCTION

Much can be said on the topic of Purpose in relations to every individual having one. What seems to be easier to believe is what Oprah Winfree has often been heard saying, "Everyone has a story." So, let's begin with this in mind. I recognize a story is only completed once the writer says so. A story was written about you before your life even began in your mother's womb. (Jeremiah 1:5 & Psalm 139:13) Your lifelong story makes a book of many stories. Some of your stories have not even begun to unfold. Yet every part of who you are and the experiences you may have over your lifetime is knitted uniquely together for your purpose as much as the ligaments and bones in your body have a purpose.

Each book in The Destiny Series is designed where each title could be personally formatted around you. Instead of the titles being Identity, Purpose, Authority and Legacy, they could just as easily be titled: (Insert *Your Name* Here)'s Identity, Purpose, Authority and Legacy. Afterall, you are on the discovery of YOU and hence, discussing *your book*.

We've discussed in Identity that you have been given a certain number of days within the time continuum to live, and your time is appointed and intentional. Your best intentional life is found when you acknowledge your life's purpose. Do you know what it is yet? That's okay. You are not alone. There are millions of scores of people who do not recognize life is intentional or that it serves a purpose. Why are you here? What does it all mean? If you've asked questions like this, you are already on the way to actualizing your soul purpose. Intentionality gives your purpose power to live and lead change for yourself and others.

When you realize that your life has purpose and you begin to intentionally direct your will to partner in your purpose, chapters upon chapters begin unfolding within your life's work. There will be mystery, romance, betrayal, comedy, failure, success, self-help, and so much more. The moment you make that conscious decision that your life is more than the day to day, it is possible you will meet a season of resistance. Don't let this defeat you. It is like a new birth. Afterall, everything is really nice inside the womb. But once your will lines up with opportunity within your appointed time, there is a tremendous amount of friction: BIRTH.

When we metaphorically birth something new such as an idea, process, business; there is transition from developmental stage to active stage. Birthing is similar. The embryo continues to grow and mature until it is fully developed. Once contractions begin, there is no turning back now! That new something is gaining independence. It is the process of moving from an internal concept, thought or idea to an external action, object, product. If birthing doesn't occur, it will die in the womb and the greatness of it will die with it. However, once it is out of the birthing stages, it has an identity, and it will serve a function. That function is purpose. Chaos and pain have subsided. Work has turned to rest. You, as an individual have certain gifts and talents. To have them and never explore their possibilities is to abort the purpose within you which will lead to a life unfulfilled: A book without words.

~ Be intentional in all things. ~

Personal

Purpose

1

IDENTIFYING PURPOSE

The two most important days in your life are the day you were born and the day you found out why.

Mark Twain

If you've read Identity, the first book in this series, you likely have a better understanding of who you are and are now ready to explore your purpose or the 'why' you are. Just like there are many people with the same name, they are not the same. They live in different origins, have different families, and possibly lead quite different lives. We are not all the same and aren't intended to be the same. Our differences are to be celebrated. Just as we are not the same, we do not all have the same individualized purpose. There is specificity in creative diversity. Perhaps one could copy a Rembrandt or Van Gough, but they will not be the same because the specific technique the artists use is still quite specific to them and even still, their creative works are done and not to be again. Each of us are an artistic masterpiece all created uniquely, wonderfully and with a specific purpose in mind.

DEFINING PURPOSE

According to Marion Webster's Dictionary, purpose can be used as a noun or a verb, but more accurately a noun being used as a verb characteristically at the grammatical center of a predicate to express an act, occurrence, or mode of being for agreement with the subject. We are referring to purpose as a noun with the subject being you and yours; as Webster's defines, *a subject under discussion or an action in course of execution; something set up as an object or the end to be attained: intention, resolution, or determination.*

Intentionality defines purpose. At the point that you decide you have a purpose, you become purposeful. When you choose to do something and you follow it up with action to accomplish it, your action fulfills a purpose. There are actions and inactions that will become a collective purpose of intentionality. Having intentionality begins to move the atmosphere into agreement with your targets. In other words, intentionality gives your life purpose by bringing your mind, will and emotions into a defined partnership to which puts the intent of your heart into a mental process, in order to produce physically what your heart wants. Let's face it. You can either have a mind full or *be* mindful.

A wandering mind can lead us down a wayward path. It is when we take control of our thoughts and put them within a framework of healthy processes that our circumstances begin to produce change within our environment. We also begin to mature our will and emotions, but we gain revelation through developing behaviors that put us on a fast track to produce healthy outcomes.

Have you ever been around a friend that is always looking on the positive side of things? These friends will bring you up through their encouragement. The same is true for those who are wired for a solution-focused process. They can cut through a ton of options in mere seconds and see the end result of each of those options to avoid obstacles or detriments. Likewise, a free-form personality is great to have around when you forget how to have adventure or stimulate the creative aspects of your life. There are people who are in your life that will influence not only the decisions you make, but how you deliberate to formulate your choices.

BALANCE

When you have too many voices around you or too many thoughts it can bring utter confusion or chaos: dysfunction. Getting advice from an emotionally broken individual or from someone who is inexperienced in the area you are needing counsel is a HUGE mistake! Eve consulted with a snake *Did God really say...?* We see where that got her. Wisdom encourages getting counsel from people around you who are familiar with what you are contemplating. Intentionality requires intentionality. Limit the voices to 2-3 vested individuals. First and foremost, pray over and ask for the Holy Spirit to guide your thoughts and footsteps. Seek out a similar situation in Scripture to see what is directed. There will likely be chaos in and around major decisions, but once you make a good decision, order will follow.

Every choice has an outcome. Depending on the type of choice you make, decisions have consequences; some good, some bad. We reap the outcome of those choices. Order will need to be restored where we've made bad choices. This is established through recognizing the mistake and correcting it as best we can. As a believer my first action would be to repent to Jesus for my sinful choice and then ask Father to forgive me and to restore righteous spiritual order. If my choices hurt other people I will also ask God and those whom I've let down, disappointed, or intentionally hurt to forgive me. I may even need to forgive myself for making the mistake so I can come out from any guilt or shame. The next process is to undo the wrong choice by redirecting my intentionality to walk out the correct choice. Usually, I will begin to see immediate order re-established in my atmosphere as I activate this course of action.

GOD'S INTENTION

God had a purpose and an order to what he did from the beginning, and it's all about his plan for the end of the story. The end is in the beginning and the beginning is in the end, just like his seasons represent the wheel within a wheel principle. This is his order of creation. One thing comes out of another and into another. The seed becomes a tree which produces fruit which contains more seeds. When God begins with a man, he is creating a nation. When he creates a nation, he begins with a man. The government of God is found through the sowing and reaping of a seed. Every single seed has a purpose. It is meant to go into the ground and die so it can become something bigger, greater than what it was which produces fruit. Every creature on land can enjoy this fruit, yet the fruit has its purpose too, to provide more seed. It is the Kingdom Law of Provision and Abundance through the covenant of God through the birthright and the blessing as we discussed further in Identity.

There is purpose in everything God does. We may not understand it, for his ways confound the wise, but with our obedience we can receive the fullness of our inheritance through his Son. If you are one of the skeptics who believe that your life is purposeless and you were just placed on the earth to live, do your best and die, I want you to know that there is hope for you, and that hope is found in Jesus Christ. To know Jesus is to know his father, and to know his father is to know the hope of glory.

GOD'S ORDER

When we are not mindful to stay in the center of God's order, we can quickly become a dysfunction junction in other people's lives. This is where we need accountability. We need to know where our weaknesses are, dismantle them and get them out of our lives.

Holding on to things too long can cause dysfunction. Where is the dysfunctional junction in your life? What bin do you need to place those situations in: the trash pile or the repurpose pile? Or is it the tool I need for today's pile? Where are you?

When we're cleaning our house, we compartmentalize things where they need to go. We have things that have outlived their use that we throw in a trash bin. Perhaps we say, *Someone else could use this, so I'm going to give it away.* That item's purpose now goes on to someone new. Some things in our lives have been left by someone different, but don't really fit us right now. Do those things need to stay or go? The things to which we are emotionally attached should be first in line to examine. The level of change around us is often determined by our responsiveness to the calling of the Lord.

If we stay in communion with Father, he will restore order where the enemy sowed confusion. We might have to roll up our sleeves and do a little spring cleaning, but if we're diligent and don't stop until the work is done, we can be sure God will do his part.

Stay steadfast in your identity in Christ Jesus. Stand in your faith confident that God will restore his order. That intimacy with the Lord returns you to a place where temptation doesn't even exist, and life becomes your foundation. The Spirit will move you past every temptation. Remember, you walk in Jesus, only unrighteous choices can separate you from experiencing fullness. Begin your day in him, so as you lay your head down at night having your peace assured in him and giving you rest.

ACKNOWLEDGING YOUR PURPOSES

God will use you wherever you are if you allow him, or you can be like other people and choose not to care. You will find that throughout life some people will out-grow you. There will also be those whom you outgrow. One thing I can assure you, you will not outgrow someone if you don't begin with some goal or purpose in mind that takes you down a specific journey. You can sit there as a spectator in a life you were destined to be a player in, but no one other than you, knows what God has placed inside you.

It would be easy to stay in the routine of what we've always done, but God desires the exceptional, something that's out of the norm. He likes using something that's a little radical—and maybe even ridiculous—to shock people out of their sedentary lives. God wants to see his people walk zealously after his presence, fueled by righteous passion, bringing his kingdom on earth as it is in heaven. The hum-drum routine isn't going to cut it.

If you don't know where you're going then you're going nowhere at all. That's why I started with Identity. You can't realize your purpose until you've identified your passion. For some people, it's children, for others it could be architecture, transportation, media, strategies or logistics. I don't know what your passion is, but I bet you do, and if you're one of those few people who don't know, then it's time to start discovering. What are the things that you enjoy doing? What are things that you are passionate about? To understand what drives you is to take a reflective look at yourself.

Personal Purpose

I'm not going to choose to live my passion. To that I say, if you do not choose to live for yours, someone else will choose you to live for theirs. There is a BIG difference between passion and passivity. You can't continue on that passive path and expect to reach your purpose. You need to determine what is in you, and you need to go after it. Nobody is going to try to take your purpose, but many will try to keep you from it. So be intentional.

Job 42:2 says, *I know that you can do all things, no purpose of yours can be aborted.* We're talking about Abba Father; once he sets something in motion, it's a done deal. The God-given purpose that Crispin and I have been assigned is greater than ourselves, and one can abort it except us.

There are rules of engagement in your purpose. They are defined in Scripture. It requires submission to God and others with authority over you. Become teachable. Posture yourself for learning and ask for help from those with more experience than yourself. Next is to obey no matter how weird it sounds. Obey with focused intention. The results are not up to you. God brings the results through your cooperation in obedience. Your faith in him to do meet you in your obedience reduces the temptation to operate in any performance or striving. It keeps your hands clean and your heart pure before God. Another temptation is to jump the gun. If God hasn't spoken yet, don't move. An example of this is when the people of Israel followed the cloud by day and the cloud of fire by night. When neither moved, the Israelites camped out waiting. Waiting upon the Lord will renew your strength. It is possible the next leg of the journey will require more of you so a 'forced' rest makes room for strengthening. The temptation in rest is to avoid laziness and idleness. These two behaviors lead to lawlessness. They can cause you to place your focus in other places other than God. Our rest is communion with God.

In your place of rest, it is a good time to take inventory of tools that are no longer required and tools that may be needed for the next leg of the journey. "Out with the old and in with the new" isn't about tools as much as it is about abandoning belief systems, traditions, and programming that is no longer relevant. Stay the course and don't allow yourself to be distracted by temporary life events. As you maintain priorities, remember that even good intentions can become distractions. Allow yourself to re-align and bring balance in life through established boundaries. Make time for yourself; live, laugh, love.

STAYING INTENTIONAL

We have to remember to stay engaged with our purpose and plan to finish well so we can hear those wonderful words, *Well done good and faithful servant.* That would mean that sometimes God wants to talk to us about that last job. Even when you are sweaty from work, and you have grass stuck to you. That doesn't bother him. You may only have one assignment left to fulfill, but I urge you to do it well because your name will be on it. When you put your hands to a work, the work is blessed, and you are also. You don't know how your today could affect tomorrow.

When we understand who we (the people of God) are, we operate collectively to establish God's order in the earth as the ecclesia (as the body of Christ). Metaphorically, I might be a toe, and you a finger but we make up one body. Our intentionality of purpose can change with the move and flow of our gifts and development of those gifts within the times and seasons, but destiny serves as the targeted bullseye as God ordained it before the foundations of the heavens and the earth.

Your spirit is eternal, although your body is not. We will be reunited with our bodies when we live eternally with Jesus, but for now, we pursue our destiny in the flesh with the power of the Holy Spirit. We are going to spend eternity in one of two places: with Jesus or apart from him. There are no if's, and's or but's. This is your future, and in case you didn't know, it is your destiny. Ephesians 3:10-12 states that, *[God's] intent was that now, through the Ecclesia (Christ's body on earth), the wisdom of God should be made known to the rulers and authorities in heavenly realms, according to [God's] eternal purpose that he accomplished in Jesus, our Lord. In him and through faith in him, we may approach God with freedom and confidence.* It is through this confidence in Christ our Lord that a little mustard seed of faith develops into an oak of righteousness.

The only thing that will ever be able to stand between you and a fulfilled purpose is yourself. Just because rest is part of God's order doesn't mean we're called to be passive. Your purpose was given to you to steward, but it is ultimately God's plan for the earth. If you don't help bring it to fruition, someone else will. So stay focused on the Lord, and let his purpose lead your life.

Covenant (seed) fulfilled through your obedience (sowing) is coupled with God's reward of blessing (reaping). Its basic kingdom principle of God's government when judgment is required. God uses those who know how to walk steadfastly in their identity and celebrate their differences. These differences, when paired with God's desire and our passion, cultivate momentum and change. When you are intentional, you make better choices and achieve your intended goal.

Once we intentionally partner with God's original design, to disciple others. What does disciple mean? Discipling has to do with discipline. Through the nature of discipline, we then disciple. According to the root meanings of discipline, there are two aspects to this word. One definition has to do with a training that corrects, molds, or perfects moral character. Yes, we are disciplined by God, parents, teachers, bosses, government, etc. It is in the nature of worldly existence. Another aspect of the word is an orderly conduct of obedience or pattern of behavior. In order to be disciples, we become partners in God's covenant to fulfill our part of the contract in the earth. We govern. Let's refer to what Jesus tells us to do in Matthew 10:7-8 & 28:19-20:

GO MAKE DISCIPLES

I love this part of scripture, because it activates the apostolic gift within and without. The initiation starts with you doing something. Go make disciples. If you always wait on someone or for conditions to be perfect, they may never be. As a kingdom disciple yourself, you determine change. We are in the world but not of the world. Therefore, do not exclude the world from the lifestyle disciplines of believers. Show them, as an example, what upright living is to be. Furthermore, Jesus tells us that he does what his Father says to do. You don't have to muster any super strength. You just be yourself, while maturing in the nature of Jesus, just as he demonstrated the nature of his Father. God's covenant with you will bring the change, you simply obey and go make more disciples. This is God's government on the earth referred to as the ecclesia. This was the original intent for the body of believers.

PROCLAIM!

Let others know that the kingdom of heaven has come. Mark 10 is giving us a depiction of the 'now' message as Jesus was among them. Prophesy what has been spoken as revelation comes to you through your maturation in discerning God's voice for now. He hasn't stopped speaking to his people. He speaks to us in many different ways, but because historically we've traveled so far from His original intent, we've not rightly heard or seen the move of God in our midst. This is why we need the gifts of the prophets, so we can rightly know God's times and seasons among us.

BAPTIZE THEM

There are two baptisms, physical and spiritual. This is symbolic of the external change that people see through our disciplines and the internal change that is within where our choices are governed by the Spirit in obedience to Father. This is active participation of discipleship through evangelizing. Whether discipling or evangelizing at work or home, you should see the fruit of your labor there. Change happens when we become missionaries to take the truth where we go.

TELL THE NATIONS

Tell all nations what exactly? Truth. It is provided by the written and spoken word of God. God's word is powerful. It is transformative. It is authority. It is also demonstrated through His only son, Jesus. Then it is replicated by his disciples because they do as Father and Son. This is where the gift of teacher comes in. The truth must be given with purity and clarity in Holy Spirit. The message that the kingdom of God is here still remains in the earth, and is done through his people, the living active harvest. Some versions of scripture tell us to *teach them to obey all that is commanded*. Disciple them in discipline.

MOBILIZE

Heal the sick, raise the dead, cure those with disease, and drive out demons. According to Jesus' words in Matthew 10:8, our deliverance from sin and transgressions didn't cost us anything. Jesus already paid the price that *all* should be made free. Therefore, utilizing a gift of the pastor, we tend to the infirmed and broken. What causes disease, infirmity, oppression, or possession? Scripture says that these things come upon us through sin, transgression, and iniquities.

Sin is something done through a willful decision, or a decision made in ignorance to the understanding of God's commands. Sin against God in relation to his covenant with us is directly connected to the first four commandments. This means we have not kept up our end of relationship.

Transgression is also sin in relation to the breaking of God's laws that affect man and his relationship to others. It is a direct violation against God and his covenant with mankind. Typically transgressions are referring to commandments five through ten.

Iniquity is a gross injustice through wickedness. This often occurs through the generational lines when there is a partaking of witchcraft, occult, or the celebrations of traditions for occult rituals. In coming into agreement with these traditions through celebration, one comes into covenantal agreement with the kingdom of darkness. One doesn't have to knowingly commit an animal or human sacrifice, but one becomes guilty by association through the power of agreement.

The blood of Jesus brought us back into a covenant with Father which costs us nothing. In order to function freely in God's

Identifying Purpose

Kingdom, we need to be saved, healed, and delivered. The freer we become, the more mature we will be to move throughout the kingdom with kingdom authority. Functioning with intentionality in the disciple of God's order, the blessings that abound through covenant affect your legacy of prosperity. Jesus sowed seed in your inheritance that benefits you and his kingdom as you reap through covenant.

INITIATION OF PURPOSE

This week your Purpose study guide will address some practical tools to organize your life for intentionality. There are likely things this week that you may already know, perhaps some you didn't. But hold on. The best information contained in these chapters are concepts and tools that have rarely been actualized together anywhere else, if at all. The ability to be able to formulate this material the way I have is a gift design unique to myself, part of my purpose, if you will. I am all too thrilled to share it with you. Think of this book and the study guide metaphorically as a DNA strand that is uniquely woven together, containing protein codes that are embedded within to assist you in your purpose according to God's grand design. My hope is that you see how it all fits together in this thing called life and it will propel you in your purpose.

Purpose was initiated in God and with God. Therefore, the journey cannot be fully actualized if you are not willing to surrender to his ultimate plan. Everything about you is built from his foundation according to who you are capable to become in him. Can you get through life without his purpose leading your life? Yes. This is why he gave you free will. He wants you to choose to do life with him. This was his original intent for your life. He can fulfill his purposes on earth without you. But he would rather do it with you. Are you ready?

2

PURPOSE OF CHARACTER

When we have a wrong understanding of our identity, it causes dysfunctions in our purpose. Our identity is found in he who created us in his own image. When we are reborn through the power of the Messiah, we begin to shed the old identity in order to reflect more of our new eternal identity. The purpose that we had been operating under before is also restored to its original intent. Our initial baby-steps contain two simple directives: First, God is God, therefore have no other gods. Jesus said to love God with all our heart. If and when we love someone, we show them honor. We make them a priority. God is the ultimate priority of all things. Secondly, love our neighbors as ourselves. God gives in his commandments five through ten, instructions on how to treat others. He establishes that how we treat others is at the bedrock of honor.

Relationships are extremely important to God. Honor for one another makes room for love. Honor requires discipline. Discipline requires obedience. You can obey without honor, but you cannot honor without obedience.

Amid an intense schedule, a sudden change of plans around my daughter's bridal shower brought on a frenzy juggling deadlines. Somehow work responsibilities didn't validate missing her only bridal shower. I had faith that God would supply the provision for me if I went.

I prepared my daughter by informing her any spare time would be dedicated to a working weekend. My daughter told me in sincerity she understood and was thankful that I would be there to share this important moment in her life. This was mutual honor.

Purpose of Character

My children are part of my purpose, and as such, a priority in my life. It was a beautiful visit. There was so much of God in it. There was no guilt in temporarily abandoning the work, but I did wonder how I would manage to be prepared on time. My heart was to be a good steward to the speaking engagement that needed preparation while being present for my daughter's bridal shower. Once I arrived home to complete my work, everything turned out better than I could have imagined. It's like God stretched time for me to fit in everything in order to honor each well. This was a big deal. He allowed me to show honor due to my daughter and still honor the work he placed in my hands. He restored everything back to me through honor. All of it was completed with time to spare. This is the blessing of the Father. This is a testimony of what has been demonstrated in my life. This is how God demonstrated to me that if I honor those around me, he will honor me.

HOW WE HONOR

Honor is integrity. Maintaining our spiritual integrity is part of how we honor God. It's not so much about what we do in front of people, but those things we do when nobody's watching. Are you looking over your shoulder? If you are, there's probably some spiritual compromise in your life and you're opening a door to something that you will most likely regret.

Do you notice those people around you who only do 80% of a job? Or the ones who take a pen home from work because the company has a million of them? Honor is the way you conduct yourself when you're only with yourself. How many times do people return or pay for what they have taken? Most people would say it doesn't matter, but as a businesswoman, trust me, it does. When you steal from corporations, it ultimately comes back to the employees. People lose their jobs. Honor is a serious matter.

To steal is to dishonor, that's why it's one of the commandments. *Thou shall not steal.* If I were to steal not only am I robbing myself of a blessing, but I am also dishonoring somebody else. Have you ever heard anyone say, *Well, they don't deserve it anyway?* Who gets to decide that? We do not get to decide who is worthy and who is not. Judging leads us towards a pitfall because it's pride, and pride goes before a fall. Our responsibility is to honor. Calvin Coolidge said, "No person was ever honored for what he received. Honor is the reward for what he gave."

Jesus gave his life, and therefore, deserves all our honor. He gave his everything for crimes he never committed, and yet, the name of Jesus is the most misused name in the world. Honor for someone is not only reflected through actions, but also in our words.

Your nation's military is worthy of honor because they serve the people for the protection of your nation. If someone burns their nation's flag, it disparages the sacrifices that nation's military has made. Moreover, burning the flag also heaps dishonor upon the one who burns the flag. We shouldn't take sacrifices for granted, especially ones you may not be willing to make. Likewise, we shouldn't take salvation for granted either.

When I was preparing this chapter, Crispin said, *Why don't you talk about sons and daughters?* This suggestion struck me so profoundly that I thought it had to be divine revelation.

When we had our children, they didn't start out making the financial decisions or planning the menus for the household. Crispin and I made those decisions. But with time and maturity, they began to work with us in those areas of governing our home. Later, when our children started driving, guess what? Sometimes they had to go and pick up one of their siblings or a gallon of milk. They didn't start out with the keys, but once they proved themselves capable with small responsibilities, like making their beds or cleaning their rooms, we trusted them more. We didn't let them have their own rooms until they demonstrated that they could maintain them. If they couldn't handle their own space, we made them share.

We weren't only teaching them responsibility and how to honor their parents through obedience, we were teaching them how to serve.

Purpose of Character

Let me be clear: children are not servants, but we are to mentor them into their own responsibilities so that they can begin to master and rule over things in their own lives. Every ruler starts out as a servant, and every ruler should know how to serve. From the day your child is born you fix every meal for them, cut their meat and clean up after them, make their bed, lay their clothes out, wash their laundry and a million things between, so that they will be ready to move out on their own as independent adults when they have grown. But when they are young, they can't live independently because they haven't learned how to serve yet. A person has to learn how to serve themselves before they can serve others.

Children have to get up and brush their teeth, do chores around the house, and finish their homework. They are honoring those who have served them while being taught to serve themselves. When they do what honors the home, you had better make sure you attend their ball game, they have a clean uniform, and celebrate a game well played- perhaps with some sort of refreshment. There is service on both sides. By instilling in our children a willingness and capacity to serve themselves, they learn how to serve others. It's not captivity, it won't hold them down, it's a tool to help them grow and become independent.

Many people don't like the term "servant." They think it means being less than someone. They don't see the beauty in servitude. Jesus came to do little else than serve a people he created. He served his father and he served humanity. That was his purpose, and I think that if the son of God was humble enough to honor through serving, then we are without excuse.

Submission is the foundation of obedience. If a child obeys, but says in his heart, *I'm not obeying on the inside*, this leads to a rebellious spirit and will inevitably lead to defiance. Defiance removes that child outside of the protection of their parents. A father desires his children to be well and thrive. When a child cheerfully obeys, not only do they remain under the protection that obedience brings them, but a blessing is involved. Go back and read

Personal Purpose

what Scripture says about the fifth commandment. It is the first commandment with a covenantal blessing attached to it.

SERVING IS A GIFT

As believers, we are called to serve just as Jesus did. This is where "love your neighbor as yourself" comes in. Service is a gift, not only to the recipient but also to yourself and your Father in heaven.

You can serve wherever you are. God gave you a job so that you can serve in a capacity for that job. You're to go in with praise on your lips because part of your livelihood is being provided through the service that you're willing to give. Your economy then improves as a result of your diligence, and when that service is not available anymore, your economy is going to suffer, right? Therefore, when I work for my employer from a posture of servanthood, it is my responsibility to do my work with excellence. I have this responsibility because I represent Jesus and he served better than anyone. God honors our service to others.

Laban, the father-in-law of Jacob, took full advantage of Jacob in the book of Genesis. He dealt with his son-in-law dishonorably, but Jacob never dishonored him in return. He worked for seven years without pay for the promise of Laban's daughter, Rachel, only to find on his wedding night that he had been given the older daughter, Leah. When Jacob confronted Laban about this, I imagine Laban saying something like, *You go ahead and enjoy your honeymoon with Leah. We'll reconvene a week from now, and I'll promise to give you Rachel, but in return, I want another seven years.* Jacob didn't have to honor that word. He could have taken Rachel and Leah and gone back to his father's land. But instead, he honored his word and stayed with the man who cheated him.

Laban wanted another seven years out of Jacob because he saw that everything Jacob did was blessed. But it wasn't about how his father-in-law treated him. God was getting ready to break open the storerooms of blessing that had been promised through Jacob's grandfather. But Jacob didn't realize that his obedience was setting him up for that abundant blessing. And God says, *You know what?*

Purpose of Character

Go ahead and be who I've called you to be. I'm going to unlock abundance in your life, and Laban is going to pay the price, not you. And so they marked the livestock, and Jacob ended up with the abundance. God vindicated him, and he reaped the rewards of honoring.

CHOOSING TO SERVE

When you honor others, it doesn't matter what they do to you, God will vindicate you. It is not your responsibility to defend yourself or have the last word. When you do a favor for somebody, don't think about how they will forget in a week, go ahead and do the favor out of the goodness in your heart not expecting a favor in return. That is showing honor, even if they don't show you any in return.

We are supposed to bring honor to ourselves and others; it doesn't matter what they choose to do with it. You go ahead and plant the seeds. Father sees you, and he's going to bless you. It's not an accident that the very first commandment is, honor the Lord your God. Honor him. Put his name first. Worship him. It's all about his honor and adoration. Honoring others is actually a form of honoring God, and when you do that, he takes care of you.

We slip from being a servant to a slave when we fall into negative thinking and dishonor. *I hate this job. I can't stand my boss. Let me tell you what he just did. I just wished they appreciated me.* I'm not saying your grievances don't matter, I'm just wondering where your joy went. Where's the heart to say, *I know that God provided this job for me, and if it's not working out with this boss, something else is going to work out. I know I can turn to the Father when there has been an injustice and he will vindicate me.* This should be the attitude of our hearts and the confession of our mouths.

I once had a job where my boss would go on such terrible fits of rage that I could hear him screaming and cursing all the way from the opposite end of the building. I tried to bury myself in work and just focus. I didn't know why I was at that job, but God used it, and I ended up putting some seeds in places I would have never imagined. You never know what God's doing with where he's placed you. But when it's time to shake the dust off your feet and move on, you better have left behind a legacy of honor, even in a place that was difficult.

My boss was a dishonorable man, and it would have been easy for me to slip into dishonor with him, but I had to remember that dishonor brings dishonor, but honor begets honor. So if I dig my heels in, bite my tongue, and say, *No, I'm not going to make that comment. I'm not going to be judgmental. I'm going to keep my hand to the grindstone and do what the Lord has called me to do in this season*, then my honor will give birth to more honor.

SERVANT OR SLAVE

You get to decide if you're going to be a servant or slave in this life. Nobody can put you in captivity without your permission. Let me give you an example.

Before there was a boy named Joseph, there was a great-grandfather named Abraham. Abraham made a covenant with God. God foretold that the seed of Abraham would serve in bondage for about four hundred years.

Some generations later, Joseph, the son of Jacob and Rachel was born. Joseph had a gift to dream dreams of prophetic value. The boy was favored by his father and his older brothers despised him. When Joseph shared a dream he'd received regarding his future prosperity, the brothers grew angry. Instead of killing Joseph, the brothers sold him into slavery. Joseph may've been enslaved, but he didn't become a slave. He knew someday his dream would become a reality, so he humbled himself to serve his master. He may have been enslaved, he refused to become a slave. He served with honor and regarded his masters. This honor elevated him into a position of leadership with a large amount of favor and authority.

Later, Joseph was imprisoned for a crime he didn't commit. He was kind to other prisoners and helped them in their time of need. He used his gift to interpret dreams of his prison mates which later opened a door of freedom for Joseph.

God used the very gift that provoked Joseph's brothers to betrayal to place Joseph exactly where God intended him all along.

Purpose of Character

God used the mistakes of others and a man with a heart of honor to accomplish what was supposed to be regardless of the path. *God will do what he plans to do.*

In Joseph's humble stature of servitude, he became a mighty leader. Joseph interprets Pharaoh's dream and Joseph directs Pharaoh with a plan to implementation. Pharoah insists on having Joseph at his side. Joseph didn't let his lowly position restrict him from the blessing of God, instead he used it as an opportunity to smooth over some rough edges in his heart. He humbled himself before God and served righteously so that when elevation came, he had the integrity to steward it. Joseph became the highest leader under Pharaoh. From then on, everything Joseph set his hand to prospered.

After interpreting a dream for Pharaoh, Joseph was given the keys to the kingdom, and he was unlocking every door.

God vindicated Joseph for his honor and restored broken relationships. Through this famine, Joseph's brothers came to Egypt, and Joseph was able to reconcile with them and restore the family. If Joseph would have become a bitter and resentful slave, he would not have fulfilled what God originally intended to do through him. God still would've fulfilled his promise to Abraham, but God would have used another. God has plenty of time since he's the author of time. We honor God in servitude when we honor his timeframe. It is a great lesson in honor and servitude.

Joseph's brothers didn't realize a curse had passed on through them. They stayed in Egypt growing and multiplying until there were so many of them that the Egyptians began to fear their power. They began to persecute the Hebrews because of their favor. There were enough of Jacob's descendants that they could have overcome the Egyptians, but they didn't. In fact, they started to imitate the dishonor that the Egyptians showed them.

They grumbled and complained, cursed and hated their oppressors. There was no honor found in the Hebrews towards their captors, nothing of the respect Joseph showed in Potiphar's house. God sent Moses to deliver them because they didn't recognize honor anymore. They didn't even recognize who God was anymore. Sure, they kept his commandments, but their hearts were far from him—some of them even worshiped other gods.

Even when Moses delivered the people from bondage, they couldn't shake off the slave's mindset. God couldn't offer them the fruit of his covenant because they refused to abandon their mindset of slavery. God wouldn't allow that to go into the promised land of honor because there was no honor in them. He had to wait until the right generation came along to take the land and carry the name of the Lord. When we serve with excellence, God honors our efforts. He will send an opportunity. He will open the way for blessing and honor to be restored back into our lives. He will typically use us to do it but the key to unlocking the purpose within is possessed in the attitude of our heart. Will you serve him with honor? Are you willing to serve others in honor?

SERVE AS ONE

There is no one greater than another in the body of Christ. We are equal. We each require the same saving grace to be a part of God's kingdom. We all require the same innocent blood to be shed to erase our sins. We work together in God's kingdom to achieve God's purposes. We all have different responsibilities and callings, but the body of Christ is called to work together to pursue our purposes with excellence in the appropriate times and seasons. There will be people that come through with a slave mentality, but they won't last long. They do not have honor and they do not recognize the gift of where they've been placed. They were elevated to a place of provision and eating well, but couldn't recognize it, so they fell away.

This happens all the time in the body of Christ. You have some that come along and say, *Oh, yeah, I can do this*, but then they become filled with negativity. They murmur and complain and can't see the good that's in front of them; the provision of the Lord might as well be a pig trough. Faulty vision and a wrong identity can poison the calling of the Lord on your life. Only two men entered the promised land that had traveled out of Egypt with

Moses. Joshua and Caleb were the only two with the right identity. The rest of Israel were of a new generation.

Sometimes it is that simple. We think we're supposed to be one thing or in one place, but because we're out of sync with our true calling and identity, it causes friction with our purpose, and we slip into dishonor. It may even cost us our destiny.

A long time ago Crispin and I had an opportunity to go to Nashville. We thought the timing was right, so we shook the Mobile dust from our feet and moved up there. As soon as we arrived, a strange thing started to happen. About an hour after Crispin would arrive at work he'd get a migraine. After about two weeks of this, he got the idea that something was wrong.

If Crispin says something's wrong, I don't ask questions. I grabbed my phone and called up a few of my intercessor friends and informed them that we have to know what to do by 10:00 am same day. If we were not in God's plan, then we needed to figure out what was his plan; quickly. About 9:45, I got a call from a pastor from Wichita Falls, Texas. He said, *I would really like to talk to Crispin. I think he needs to come and interview here. Come and stay about a week?*

Was this our answer? I thought we might be able to sneak in a weekend. But a week? Are you kidding me? To stay that long would definitely close the door on Nashville but what if Texas didn't work out? I could feel the Holy Spirit surrounding me; my knees started knocking the cabinet in front of me. I blurted out, *Are you sure you are hearing from God?* I figured if he were absolutely sure this would definitely eliminate our risk. In his gentle nature, he assured me he was quite confident he had. His voice settled my spirit and I responded we'd get back with him before the end of the day. I immediately called Crispin and we agreed. Something had to give. We wanted to be where the Lord wanted us.

We had only just arrived in Wichita Falls and already we knew what we were supposed to do. We'd been pursuing our purpose, but in the wrong location. So, we headed back to Nashville a little nervous at the thought of facing such a big move and having to admit we made a mistake moving back to Nashville. It didn't

Personal Purpose

matter. There was such a burning inside knowing that we had found where the Lord wanted us. We felt like it would be dishonorable to give our final acceptance without talking to our Nashville pastor first. It was the hardest thing we had ever done. We were still young—I didn't even have gray hair yet—and I think we really did look like kids.

We went into the pastor's office and had one of the toughest conversations we've had to this day. We confessed to making a mistake. We were not meant to be in that church at that time, even though we felt called there. Timing is everything and ours was horrible. *Will you forgive us? If you ask us to stay, all we can tell you is that this isn't where we're supposed to be.*

The pastor looked up at us with the blood draining from his face and said, *What you did today is the most courageous thing I've seen anyone do.*

We had come expecting him to be furious. Instead, we left humbled by his character. We knew this man and honored him; the last thing we wanted to do was burn bridges. Then he said, *I don't want you here if God's not in it. So I'll bless and release you.* Then he prayed with us, and we left the office feeling better than we had in a long time.

Honor begets honor. Our act of honoring the Lord's will for our lives and our pastor allowed us to go into an experience that fueled our ministry like it never had been before. We came up against the powers of darkness in ways that we had never experienced in our ministry before, but it was all leading up to new depths of purpose. It was a time of promotion through spiritual maturity. We even took part of that experience back with us to Nashville when it was time.

We wouldn't have had any impartation for Nashville until we went to Texas. We had to receive new training and equipment. Sure, we could do music and some other ministries, but that was not our purpose. We had to go through Texas to pick up that piece that we would carry with us back to Nashville. That was our purpose. We had to be in the right time for that season. However, had we done it in a way that didn't honor that pastor, we could have interfered with the work God wanted to do through us. We had made a mistake with where we were located, but mistakes happen. The Lord is always faithful to forgive and nudge us into right standing in pursuit of our purpose.

PROMOTION

God is looking to see how you deal with your mistakes, because there is promotion coming on the other end of your repentance and obedience. He's wanting to bless you, vindicate you, but he can't do that if you make choices that are dishonorable.

Are you a slave or a servant? It's your choice. Even a king serves his kingdom. Yes, you are sons and daughters of God, but you serve in his house and on his land. It's his. He owns the cattle on a thousand hills, and he owns the hills, too. He's entrusted what is his to us and watches to see if we're going to honor it and honor him.

Now, I don't know if you remember this from the old testament, (II Kings 5) but Elisha was a servant of Elijah. You know what that meant? He was being discipled. He was a son, and he was getting ready to be placed into his sonship.

Elijah trained young prophets. Before Elisha, Elijah had another servant. However when Jezebel was making her threats, the prophet in training slipped away at the first sign of danger. God already had someone in mind to serve Elijah. It was Elisha. When the time came that Elijah was to be carried up to heaven, he said to Elisha, *Stay here. I don't know what this 'called up' thing looks like, but it could be ugly.*

But Elisha said, *Oh, no. I will serve you until the end.*

Elijah tried persuading him again. *Now, I'm serious this time. Stay here and hold down the fort while I'm gone. Make sure the horse doesn't get away.*

Elisha probably responded something like, *The horse can come along. You can leave my side but I'm not leaving yours.*

Personal Purpose

Elisha not only loved the older prophet he also wanted his blessing. He stayed until the very end and God heard his heart. When that cloak fell, Elisha caught it, was like God said, *NOW is your promotion.* That cloak didn't just have the anointing of Elijah on it anymore, it was blessed with a double portion. His honor led to his promotion.

Naaman was the commander of the army for the King of Aram—another kind of servant—and he had his issues of leprosy. The man was a walking powder puff, if you touched the sore places on his skin, it caved in like ash. He was slowly falling apart, and there was nothing anyone in his land could do for him.

One day he heard of a great prophet in Israel who worked miracles by his God, and he knew he had to find him, regardless of what god he worshiped. So he sent his servants to bring Elisha to heal him. When Elisha heard the servants' request, he basically said, *Okay, tell him to go dip in the Jordan seven times.*

Now, you have to understand that Naaman was a man of prestige. Bathing in a dirty river was beneath him. Nevertheless, there's something about the threat of death that makes even the proudest man humble himself. He dipped seven times in the water and emerged completely healed. His years were reversed. He was restored.

In II Kings 5:15, Naaman and all his attendants went back to the man of God, stood before him, and said, *Now I know that there is no God in all the world except in Israel.* The whole process was a test. Naaman was fishing for the one true God, and he found him. Then when he saw the power of the Lord, he said to Elisha, *Please accept a gift from your servant.*

The prophet answered, *As surely as the Lord whom I serve lives, I will not accept a thing.* Naaman urged him further, but to no avail.

Had he accepted those gifts, it would have brought reproach on Elisha's ministry, and it would have disrupted his proficiency in his purpose. It would have created a wall between him and God. The gifts would have been impure. God was saying, *I am your gift. I*

Purpose of Character

am your provision. Do not rely on the strength or wealth of man. I am your portion. By refusing, Elisha was showing him not only that God worked the miracle, but that he was able to take care of his basic needs and reward him in time. The Lord returns honor for honor.

Elisha's servant Gehazi, on the other hand, did not carry himself as honorably. He thought Elisha had been too easy on the pagan general. He thought it was a terrible shame to refuse so much wealth, and he conjured a scheme to run after Naaman and say that his master changed his mind about that whole reward situation.

This is a man training to be a prophet of the most-high God, and he was preparing a deception in his mind by usurping the authority of Elisha. Gehazi went behind his master's back and did what his selfish heart desired, deception and dishonor. He intended to do the opposite of what Elisha had already established knowing that it would bring reproach on the ministry.

So Gehazi hurried after Naaman and spoke his first lie: *My master sent me.*

Now his deception had gone from his mind to his lips. What happens when a prophet speaks deception? It is false prophecy, witchcraft. This is one of the greatest temptations of a prophet, to use their words for personal gain. They must guard what they say, because if it comes out wrong, it can be misconstrued as false prophecy. That's why the enemy loves to twist words; he loves stumbling blocks.

Then Gehazi tells his second lie. *My master and two men from the company of the prophet have sent me after you.*

Now he not only does himself dishonor, but he takes two men with him from the company of the prophets (verse 22). This is just like the spirit of Jezebel. She was a false prophet, and she always had others go with her to do her dirty work. The same spirit operated within Gehazi. The deception, the false prophecy, the lies, and trying to entangle other prophets in his wickedness.

He had his two accomplices carry the loot back to his house and then he hid it. Anytime you have to hide something, there's

Personal Purpose

deception present. Never mind the rebellion—another form of witchcraft. He was rebelling against the word of Elisha, and he was foolish enough to think he could hide something from God.

When Gehazi went back to Elisha, the prophet asked where he had been. Gehazi quickly replies that he hadn't gone anywhere. Now he's just bold-faced lying to his master and mentor. Elisha is a prophet. He already saw what happened, he's just giving Gehazi the opportunity to repent. You can't hide stuff from a true prophet. Elisha called him out on what he did. *Was not my spirit with you when the man got down from his chariot to meet you? Is this the time to make money, to take money or to accept clothes or olive groves or any of these things?*

Can you imagine the color draining from Gehazi's face when Elisha said that? You can't hide deception for long without God shining a light on it. This is what happened next: Elisha said, Naaman's leprosy will cling to you and your descendants, *Gehazi, because of what you have done today. Because you usurped the authority. Because you brought reproach on my character while leading two of my servants into deception.* Gehazi then fled from Elisha's presence, his skin white as snow.

If we dishonor authority—if we dishonor God—we bring reproach upon ourselves. Do you see what Gehazi was going to bring on Elisha's purpose? Instead, he brought the curse upon his own life and his descendants instead of Elisha. The Old Testament says that when you have a rebellious son, take him before the city and stone him. While we don't stone anyone today, rebellion breeds dishonor and is not to be taken lightly. The Scripture actually says it leads to witchcraft, or wicked character. You need to know when you set your mind to deceive that you are bringing curses upon yourself and your descendants. Yes, we have Jesus, we have the blood, but if we don't see the reproach on our lives, we can still struggle with generational issues.

I have often wondered in my own life, *Where did that dishonor take place in the generational line?* Jesus is like the Jordan River, he's the water that washes over my soul. He paid the price, and it was his honor to lay himself down. Therefore, to turn away and deny every wicked thing is to honor God. Recognizing his authority in our life and submitting to a life of obedience makes room for promotion. Before you can rule, you must learn to serve. If you can learn how to serve when there's just one or two people, eventually you'll serve many — you'll serve a kingdom.

HONOR TO SERVE

Joseph had many people under his rule — an entire nation, actually — but he still had authorities above him to honor. I am convinced that the body of Christ must be known for its honor if we are to walk into our inheritance. Even when people aren't looking. Gehazi thought no one was watching, but God knew his heart, and it was given testament in the word. Your heart and your thoughts are being recorded. Yes, God's mercies are new every morning, but be aware that even though he is faithful to forgive, you do not want to bring his judgement against you. That doesn't mean we escape the punishment. It just means we're not suffering unto death. But there is a reaping for disobedience. There is a reaping for dishonor.

That's why I pray that in all I do, I honor the Lord. I may have moments where I fall into dishonor, but I repent quickly and thank God that I cannot exhaust his mercy. My heart is to honor, not only God, but everyone I come in contact with, and that is a purpose we are all called to do with excellence.

There are other ways to express honor as well. It has to do with thinking about the results of the unknown. For example: It's honorable just to put your shopping buggy away when you empty your cart into your vehicle. You know why? Because someone may need the parking spot a buggy was left in. It also prevents it rolling into somebody's car leaving a big scratch or dent. As a customer, I appreciate the honor my grocer demonstrates in making sure fresher produce is available. It's the little things.

God has a way of demonstrating his kingdom principles through events in our lives to produce spiritual maturity or "perfection" as Scripture calls it. Honor becomes the mortar that holds those experiences together. When this perfecting of kingdom

Personal Purpose

principles occurs throughout a region, a new culture develops bringing God's perfect order. We call this culture the Kingdom of God and its occupants the ecclesia. This culture of distinction represents a kingdom identity synonymous with God's purpose.

3

*P*URPOSE OF *D*ISTINCTION

Matthew 7:11 says that even evil people want to give their children gifts, but moreover our heavenly Father, who is good, gives good gifts to his children, if you ask. As we trust in Father's goodness, we begin to experience more relationship with him. We want to experience more of his kindness. James 1:17 says that every good and perfect gift originates with Father. Therefore, we can trust that he only gives gifts that will be good for us and others. If we can trust that God gives good gifts, then we can trust that his son, Jesus does also.

There are so many gifts of the Father, they cannot be counted. Scriptures give us glimpses of certain types of gifts that we discussed in more detail in Identity, but we are not to stop there. We come into submission to our covenantal relationship with Jesus, our kingdom ruler, to achieve the heart of His Father. Three types of gifts we discovered were the redemptive gifts of Father given at birth, the fivefold gifts, discoverable as we come into salvation through the remittance of since through the atoning blood of Jesus as a spiritual birth, and the manifestation gifts that flow as a result of Holy Spirit through the seven Spirits of God that come as we mature and sanctify ourselves producing the fruits of the Spirit. Jesus said in John 12: 24-26, a grain, *kernel of seed*, of wheat must go into the earth and die so it may bring forth much fruit, *harvest, or offspring*. The Greek word for fruit is *karpos (G2590)* in Strong's Concordance which means actual fruit; as the fruit of trees, vines, or field, and of one's loins such as progeny or posterity. Another definition for fruit is that which originates from something else as a result, such as praise to God as a thank offering, or some form of work, act, or profit, utility, reaped harvest, or gathered fruit which giving a connotation of eternal life or something without an end.

Personal Purpose

Again let me reiterate: The government of God is established with a seed through covenant and is demonstrated through the kingdom principle of sowing and reaping as God's judgment whereby as a man thinks (sows) so is he (does he reap) as written in Proverbs 23:7. Birthright is the covenant that God will provide. Blessing is the reward of abundance, more than provision because of obedience and your active participation in God's covenant. The land is in this covenant with you because God created it as a provision. Therefore, the resources of the land belong to you and will yield fruit because its purpose was to provide for you as you honor your covenant with God. The abundance of the animals on the land and the ability of supply of commerce are the manifestations as a witness of covenant between you, God, and the land. It is all Kingdom Principle because God established his government in the earth from the beginning. Jesus came to restore that covenant through his atoning blood and so we must continue in his purpose to honor the covenant.

GIFTS OF DISTINCTION

In Ephesians 4:11, the Apostle Paul tells us that Jesus gave gifts to the body of believers for some to be apostles, prophets, teachers, evangelists, and pastors. This is what is commonly known as the fivefold ministry—five gifts in the Lord's ecclesia. The ecclesia includes those who gather to determine the heart of God as a demonstration of God in the earth. We are in this world, but not of this world. We are to be set apart, as a peculiar people, but we were never designed to exclude ourselves from the demonstration of God within us throughout the world. This Scripture and concept are important, I want you to wrap your whole spirit around it like a closed fist. This is where the Church is headed, whether they're on board or not. Your purpose is intertwined with your fivefold gifting, and you walking in that to your fullest is God's heart for you. It is up to you to ask Jesus to impart these and fulfill these gifts within you for the purpose of his kingdom. You are able to have all five, but it has to be developed similarly to your prayer language and stewarded just like your seed, land, and livelihood or better understood as the birthright and blessing of Father through covenant.

All throughout the Church you will hear people saying that parts of the fivefold do not exist in our modern world. *The apostles are not for today,* some will say. *Prophets died with the Old Testament;* others will attest. This is part of the enemy's plan to stifle the movement of God. All of the fivefold gifts are both present and necessary in the body of Christ. This may shock you: If you can discern (hear) God's voice, then you have the ability to prophesy. That may not make you a prophet, but it is a living demonstration of one of the fivefold within because you have the ability to hear God's voice for yourself and do exactly what he tells you to do. The same applies to the other four.

SET APART BUT NOT WITHDRAWN

Why are people leaving the church? Why has church left the building? Unfortunately, doctrine and philosophy have tainted the purity and integrity of scriptures. When we do this, as individuals or as a community, it diminishes the effectiveness of our spiritual growth and hinders our purpose. One example of this is shown through the dismissal of the necessary aspects of the fivefold. Many churches are not teaching or exercising the gifts of God. They are not demonstrating the kingdom of God through these gifts which bring the power of the Kingdom just as it was in the time of the disciples. How so? It would be like me telling you to survive without a lung. Yes, you can do it, but eventually other systems of the body will become weakened and compromised because the body needs two fully functioning lungs. That's why God gave us two.

Everything we do is the result of choices with results that follow. The question remains, are our choices motivated by God's purpose or our own? What is the motive of your heart? You have already been given everything you need through the covenantal provision of God. He gave his spoken and written Word as an example of how to live a life fulfilled. Recognizing that our gifts were intentionally delegated to us as a particular DNA code for a

Personal Purpose

specific region of the world through a book about you already spoken before the foundation of the world helps us realize that the free will we have is all about directing us back toward the relationship with One who knows us best.

Why is this important? Authority is delegated power. If you misuse your authority, you are responsible for the consequences. The responsibility has been granted through covenant, so you need to know how to function in it with honor. The Great Commission in Matthew, Jesus says , *all authority have I given you.* Did you notice how he didn't say some authority? Jesus himself demonstrated "all authority" in his three years of ministry, checking off every box of every kingdom gift. Think of an older sibling looking after the younger. As the older child grows and matures, he is given more and more responsibility. With greater responsibility comes greater accountability. Jesus knew what those three transformative years were supposed to look like and led through the apostolic blueprint as he set in motion a course that had not yet been run. He pastored his disciples. He evangelized and taught the multitudes. He prophesied his death and resurrection. He brought understanding of true liberty in obedience unto God through his teaching. He was all the fivefold rolled into one. The Great Commission is a lifestyle of the demonstration of God's gifts.

Even though it is true that we do not necessarily walk in all the gifts all the time, there are and will be times when one is more prominent than another. Our life's purpose doesn't change, but certain responsibilities or focuses within a purpose change with the times and the seasons. I was called during one season to be a mom. I still am a mother today, but I am no longer *Mom* like I was in that season, when my children clung to me and needed me around the clock. There was a time and season before motherhood when I walked through a new relationship and a new covenant as a bride. Today I am still a bride, but my walk has shifted to the point where we are more than just a young couple, we are a seasoned team closer than we've ever been. Just as our relationships and responsibilities change throughout life with the times and seasons, we are also to mature spiritually. We no longer just read the Bible as a chapter at a time as a chore, but we read it with our spirit to hear the deeper message within. We search for the deeper or meatier things of God written in the mystery of the Word.

DISCIPLINARY ACTION

Looking at the individual purposes and functions of the gifts, we have apostles that govern, prophets to help guide, evangelists to garner, pastors to guard and teachers to simplify and make relevant. How is it, then, that if we've been given all five giftings that we don't see all of them expressed? Obedience is usually the key, but I think having the discipline to practice has a larger role to play than we give it credit for. Practice requires obedience. As a young girl, I loved Jesus as my friend and Savior. I wasn't filled with Holy Spirit until I was thirteen years old. When I was filled, I started speaking in tongues right out of the gate. I was full of fresh new fire and zeal and shared my experience with everyone that crossed my path. It was like I came to life. However, I didn't really know what to do with the gift of tongues or how to use it. After going years not knowing what to do with this gift, I asked a trusted intercessor. I was told to exercise speaking in tongues in order to mature in my spiritual language. I didn't understand initially. Was I supposed to practice? This was news to me. However, it made sense because I had recently learned how to speak a foreign language in High School so I figured it must be similar to that. The only difference was that I didn't always know what I was saying in the Spirit. That too had to be developed. I now realize, I'm not always meant to know what the Spirit is saying. Sometimes the prayer language is simply meant to edify my spirit. My spirit knows and that's enough.

To practice speaking in tongues, isn't that sacrilegious? Isn't that mocking the Holy Spirit? No, it's not at all unless the intent of your heart is to mock the Spirit of God. We are to be like little children so God can teach and train us in things of which we do not have an understanding. Just like natural talents, we're stronger in some things than others. However, practice allows us to hone our skills. The same is true with the Gifts of God. Sometimes we are given gifts that are prevalent on our generational line. When you humble yourself to the Holy Spirit for maturation, as you steward your gifts well in obedience and faithfulness, you will be given more. Remember kingdom principle is to reap what is sown through the obedience of Jesus and His Spirit. As you become more about our Father's purposes, you will become more like Him in nature, acquiring good gifts, demonstrating healthy fruit character.

Growth, accountability, and practice nurture an atmosphere for mature functionality, not just as an individual, but as a community effort as the body of believers. His kingdom come on earth as it is in heaven. His will be done.

GIFT OF AUTHORITY

The Bible says that the fivefold gifts are given when we accept Jesus Christ as Lord. So why do so many believers live with half of their salvation?

Just like we read earlier in Matthew, we have been given all authority. The fivefold is the governmental authority of the Kingdom of God, therefore, if he gave us all authority, he's making us his kings and priests in this realm. The "you" Jesus was speaking happened to be the disciples, but the same applies to every believer. I can just imagine him taking them aside and saying, *I'm going to show you some things. I'm about to tell you why you're here, and why I have selected you to walk with me while I'm here.*

There were others that Jesus called, but only twelve who answered. Remember the rich young ruler? Jesus asked him to sell everything he owned and follow him, but he just wasn't there yet. I hope that he eventually got there, but maybe he didn't. There are people right now who are called to an active role in the next great move of God who are just not ready, and that's okay. It's important that they come into their identity first. Believers need to be mature in their faith with their feet firmly planted in Scripture before they move into the deeper things of God. It's not for the faint of heart. That doesn't mean that everything is a struggle, it just means that to whom much is given, much is required. Remember, Moses was exiled before he was called by God to return to Egypt.

When Paul said in Ephesians 1:3 that we have been given every spiritual blessing, he's talking to all believers, the old, the young, the faithful and the stumbling. This is part of our birthright through salvation and one of our main tools for building the kingdom that we so often overlook. We need to look past the natural, past what religion would have us think, and see with the perspective of heaven who we are and realize what we were put here to accomplish. God is not religious. He is relational and he is governmental.

It can so often be our perspective and doctrine that keeps us shackled to tradition rather than covenanted in Kingdom destiny. Just like the perspective where the church has left the building, many people are leaving because of their personal issues with the Church or how it is run. People are leaving frustrated. Some leave searching for more. But in their midst are also those who are going out into their sphere of influence and seeing the effectiveness of their obedience move those spheres toward the Kingdom of God. We don't need every believer laboring in the Church, truth be told. There are different types of believers just like there are two kinds of apostles. We had the apostles like Paul who went out, cleared the way and laid a foundation, and then those like Timothy who would come behind establishing teams, working with them and sending them out to be apostles of their own. That's kingdom multiplication at work, and it can only come by effectively wielding the authority we've been given.

GIFTS OF HARVEST

The Bible says that every good and perfect gift comes from God. Even though we all have particular areas within the gifts where we excel, we should be able to operate in any one of them when necessary. We have been given the gifts of the Father and of the Son. Those who carry them are the government of the kingdom of God. As believers, we're supposed to come to Church, get our fill and go out overflowing with seeds of harvest. You may not realize it, but you are the harvest. I am the harvest. WE ARE THE HARVEST. The kingdom of God is at hand. Can we just come together and agree on that without competition, strife, or doctrine? Because I promise you, when we pull down our walls and seek his face together, God will come in and move like never before. We're supposed to go, petal to the floor, gaining speed and momentum to see the darkness defeated through our intentionality. We are of one Spirit and should come into agreement with one another, one mind, one accord operating in covenant together. We should overcome our objections of one another to be one with His heart. We may all have our opinions, but opinions do not matter when it comes to Father's heart.

There are times I've had to adjust my moral compass. The things I wanted did not align with Father's heart. I was trying to justify my actions because there were things in my heart that suited me. Oh c'mon, you've been there too, you know it. See, that is what makes us human, but we are also spirit. The Spirit of God moves through us to establish his purpose and he uses the gifts he gives us as tools to demonstrate his love. Every gift becomes another weapon in your arsenal in winning kingdom territory or planting new fields of harvest. If we didn't have that measure Christ gave us, we wouldn't be able to work in giftings. We were each given a measure, but we have to exercise it. We have to till the soil. We cannot let the opportunities pass by. Every time I step into a new assignment that God puts before me, God gives me a new tool. No exceptions. He will always build and establish us in the gifts that he's given. When we prove, as we mature and demonstrate effective use of these gifts, that we can handle what we've been given, God opens heaven and gives us something new.

Consider Maslow's hierarchy of needs. The last of the five needs is self-actualization, which for Christians is our life fulfilled in Christ Jesus. When we recognize our identity and understand that our intentionality within our purpose changes with the times and seasons, we are actualizing our designed function. I can't give more or less without God. I can only do what he's given me, in this time, for this season. Yes, I could do less, but I would fall short of

Purpose of Distinction

my destiny through an unfulfilled purpose. Self-actualization is the realization that I am nothing without God and have everything with him.

DISTINGUISHED COUPLE

The groom, Jesus, is preparing a place for a spotless bride, his church. He is waiting for us to prepare ourselves for him. Hope deferred makes the heart sick, but I'm telling you, this is the movement that we're in, and I'll shout it to the ends of the earth. Whether two, two thousand, or two million people hear what I'm saying, I will not keep silent. God wants us operating in our full purpose to fulfill the destiny that he placed within us before the foundation of the world, to establish his kingdom and government on Earth. Jesus is ready to return to rule, but his bride is not ready to receive him. We're calling out for him to come, but he's saying that faith without works is dead. You have to get dressed. Adorn yourself for the bridegroom just as he is preparing a place for us.

Back in 2004, the Lord gave me a word while I was driving westbound on I-40. He wanted me to stop and write down this word of prophecy, but I insisted that I'd remember and kept driving. God doesn't give up that easy, so we had this intense conversation, yes - no, back and forth. It wasn't until he had a police officer pull up behind me and turn on his flashers that I got the hint and pulled over to write the word down. I'm sure God doesn't talk to anyone else like that—I'm especially hardheaded. Needless to say, I am more responsive now when he speaks than what I used to be.

The Lord wanted me to deliver a word to my local church congregation from the pulpit. I almost broke out in a sweat. *They believe in the interpretation of tongues, but I don't think they believe in prophetic words, Lord.* Either way, I could discern the conviction of the Lord and I was given instructions by Holy Spirit to deliver it, but time would be cut close. I didn't really have time to pull off and write it down. In the Lord's humor, he put a policeman behind me who turned on his lights. I thought I was being pulled over, but I

Personal Purpose

wasn't. Regardless, it startled me so much I needed to pull off anyway. I might as well obey and write the message down.

I was two and a half hours away when God gave me the word. I would gain an hour but calculated I would still be at least thirty minutes late upon arrival. I hustled through the doors, met with an elder, told him the word and braced for impact.

His reaction took me completely off guard. He looked at me thoughtfully and said something like, *Well, this message sounds like scriptures out of Isaiah 61 and Revelation 19. I can confirm this is a revelatory word from the Lord.* There was no getting out of it now. I had submitted to my spouse and church elder for prayer and consideration and I was given consent to obey. (God will provide the agreement if your church's protocols call for it. If not, contact me for counsel.)

When the time came, it took every ounce of determination I had to walk up on that platform, seize the microphone and say what the Lord had spoken to my heart. I can't remember the full word, but the gist of it has stuck with me through the years—or at least the headline. The Lord sent this message to this church: *What kind of bride sleeps during the preparation of her wedding? She adorns herself with beauty (gifts) and makes herself ready. She is not found sleeping.*

There was nothing original in this prophetic word. It was straight out of Scripture. But it struck me and everyone else in that sanctuary like fresh revelation.

The bride is supposed to make herself ready for her bridegroom while he has gone to prepare a place for her. She and her friends make preparation for the big celebration. She picks out jewels and the right dress to wear. She orders the flowers and prepares for the reception. She's governing the affair. She calls the shots because she's the bride. Jesus wants a bride who is eager to be with him, to live and rule beside him.

Jesus is ready. He's at the ready, *When I get the word, I'll come.* He will not come until everything is ready, the veil is on, and the bride sends the message, *I'm ready.*

Jesus did everything he needed to do more than two-thousand years ago. He's waiting on us to move into kingdom order. We have to move into this new work that isn't really new at all, but the unadulterated message has been buried over time. It has been buried through the harlot church under doctrine, pride, religion, and compromise. Jesus is saying in so many words, *I'm sending out a call the way John the Baptist did through my apostles, prophets, evangelists, pastors, and teachers. Tell them I'm coming, but that they must be ready for me.* Zion is prepared as we make ourselves ready in the earth. We bring the kingdom of heaven to earth through the power of Holy Spirit operating fully throughout our lives. Our responsibility, as the body of believers, is to bring kingdom order as the Ecclesia.

VINTAGE HARVEST

As we move on to the next section of Purpose, we will be talking about the governmental system that God designed in the earth for the benefit of living our best life for the kingdom of God. When you read the Old Testament of scripture, you see the development of the seed, Sower, and Reaper through Adam, Noah, Abraham, Isaac, and Israel aka Jacob. From their seed good and evil were produced in the earth. God wants us restored to our original intent. He accomplishes this through God's only begotten son, Jesus. The New Testament demonstrates the government of God as Jesus restores the kingdom of God in the earth. We refer to this as the *Ecclesia*.

Traditionally in scripture, you will see *church* as the term referenced as the assembling of believers. Assembling had its purpose. This is where the body of believers would come together to worship and commune. This was the relational aspect of assembling, that we might know one another. Please refer to John 17:22-24. This is referring to the kingdom glory being seen in the earth through us as one. Assembling for that purpose alone is not

Personal Purpose

all. The true reason is to talk about how unrighteousness is trying to infiltrate not only the personhood of individual believers such as yourself, but to divide the kingdom of God from within and without.

When I say 'within', this means inside or from within such as one's personal conscience, body, group, or government. When I say without, I am not saying in absent from or not existing but speaking of those things outside of yourself, group, or government that try to change or alter you through influence.

The Old Testament represents the first fruits of the kingdom of God and his government. First fruit is like the firstborn. It doesn't represent the entire volume of harvest, but it is the first gleaning of the harvest. For example: Having four children, the first born represents the first fruit of offspring. Mankind was not the first born of God's seed but of his hand. Adam and Eve were the first of God's government established in the Garden. God's government was taught to us through the lineage of God's covenant with man and the land that would become Israel. Its government came through the Law of the Commandments given to Moses.

The New Testament is where we read about the birthright of God's firstborn heir and learn more about how a true heir is to live and reign in the earth. Jesus is God's firstborn, birthed of his seed. His government was demonstrated through the gift of Holy Spirit and discipleship. Jesus came to fulfill the law through the relationship of love and sacrifice. Jesus came to establish his kingdom first to the Jews not just as a people group but a nation. This is governing. After Jesus ascended into heaven, the disciples were sent unto the Gentiles to disciple. The first fruit of the Gentiles was a man named Cornelius. Cornelius' entire household became born again and we see the government of God being expanded from out of the Jews and throughout. This was demonstrating how those in covenant with God are to live in the fulness of Kingdom through obedience.

The ecclesia is the government of God, who demonstrates His power and authority in love as written in John 17, utilizing the

Purpose of Distinction

fruits and gifts of Holy Spirit. The ecclesia has been labeled a long time as church, but the term 'church' doesn't make room for the government of God. Instead it usurps God's government by redirecting leadership to a manmade structure of government rather than God's. When we are filled with Holy Spirit, we occupy the kingdom of God as it dwells in us. We rule in God's kingdom by allowing Holy Spirit to operate and manifest through us. It is not we, ourselves. It is by HIS MIGHT and HIS POWER within us to flow through us. As the Ecclesia, one with Jesus and his purpose, we govern by overturning the unrighteous kingdom through the demonstration of our authority within the infrastructure of God's kingdom.

There was the first example of his government through the seed of Abraham, who became several tribes and eventually one nation. Then Jesus came and established the new government through the rebirth through salvation. He established his governmental order through the fivefold, bringing freedom to all nations of the earth through the Israelites first, and then the Gentiles.

There will be sheep and goat nations depending on whom they serve. We as representatives and heirs of God's kingdom have a duty to take dominion in the earth to subdue it from the sin, transgressions and iniquity through the power of repentance through Christ Jesus. We follow the order of Melchizedek demonstrated by Jesus as kings and priests of righteousness and peace in the earth.

ANCESTRAL PURPOSE

_4_

ORIGINAL INTENT

In the beginning was God… who was, is and always will be. The 'beginning' denotes the framework of time that had a definite initiation and a definite end within the matrix of infinity. Infinity has no beginning or end. God determined what was light and what was darkness. In the earth, are two kingdoms, the kingdom of light and the kingdom of darkness. In a day, there is light and there is dark. Light represents life. Darkness represents death. God has an order of intentionality that draws us back to him. It was, is and always will be his purpose.

The day and night are both twelve hours long. God intended the day to end and begin with the setting of the sun. Most of us have been trained that the new day begins at midnight or at the rising of the sun. This belief places us outside of God's timing. The darkness lasts for twelve hours, and then is followed by twelve hours of light. The midday point is at sunrise not noonday.

PURPOSE FOR A DAY

The first part of a new day, which begins at sunset, we take inventory of the previous day. What was accomplished, left undone, or needs to be improved upon or abandoned? This is how we spend the beginning of the new day. Then we make preparation for the rest of the day once we take our rest. We begin with rest so that our bodies can be refreshed and renewed, we've already prepared for the day, so now we spring forth into action like the sunrise. We work what has been planned diligently making the most of our time. As the day begins to set, we consider the day's actions to see how they measure up to our previous sunset's forecast. Planning and preparation produce purpose. Each day has been appointed with purpose to help us be intentional to complete what is being produced through us.

Cycles of time are the measurement we use to determine a beginning and an end. Each twenty-four-hour day not only has a half mark to divide night and day, but it also has quarter marks. This gives us the opportunity to get a pulse on our progress and make corrections if needed. The seasons follow this same pattern, two seasons winter and summer due to the revolution around the sun which also include four marked seasons in relation to earth's distance from the sun. Within these seasons are the twelve smaller seasons that are determined by the new moon, called months. Within each month are smaller cycles called days. The cycle of times and seasons is given to mark times to rest and times to work, plan and prepare.

MEDIA OF THE STARS

So day is separated from the night. Then God said, *...And let them serve as signs to mark sacred times*. The sky reflected his times and seasons as signs; there are twelve of them. All of these signs—or the Mazzaroth's—are the gospel of salvation written in the stars. Every one of them gives testimony of Jesus Christ. They are the announcement of his birth. This news not only comes through the constellations, but also through the tribes of Israel. God established a covenant with Abraham so that he could bring his son, the Seed through that covenant, to restore a new covenant with man. Adam was the first, he was in the image of God, but he wasn't the Seed of God; he was made of flesh and of the earth. As God said when he made the covenant with Abraham, *I'm going to send my seed through this covenant*.

There were two tablets in the Torah. The Word, the covenant, the promise. God said *I'm going to bring my Seed, not just what I've crafted out of my hands, my creation in my image, but now it's going to be of me*. God used the lineage of Mary to forge with the seed of the Spirit to conceive Jesus. This was his first fruits, through His Son Jesus. He was both man and God. This isn't new revelation, but this brings it all together. It's all declared in the stars. It's all declared through the tribes. Every constellation aligns with a tribe, aligning with a month. It's God's promise in the stars.

SIGNIFICANCE OF NUMBERS

Dr. Barbie Breathitt is the author of A-to-Z Dream Symbology. I don't know how many of you are dreamers. Dreams can give prophetic insights as well as lead us to prayer strategies. They speak into the direction of what is possible. Dreams also show us areas of our life that need attention. Dreams give tremendous value in being able to discern what our mind, will and emotions are entertaining. We put a lot of weight in that because we know that God talks to us through our dreams. We use Christian dream interpretation books to also evaluate what is happening in the dreams as they relate to the dates, time, and season we have those dreams. For instance, dreams during the month of Nisan may possibly give direction for the course for the rest of the year. We can only determine the relevancy of such dreams once much prayer and seeking Holy Spirit has been done. If there are other confirmations through Holy Spirit, then we acknowledge the dream isn't just about the interpretation of the dream, but about God's timing for setting something into motion. This is a time of spiritual advance, but you have to look at it from the perspective of the time of the month.

God also speaks through numbers. When you look at the clock and see repeating numbers, or a particular number keeps showing up over and over again, it is possible God is showing you something through the meaning of numbers. If you look in the Scriptures, God is a number God. He specifically named the days of the week and gave them purpose. In that purpose was given meaning. He is a detail-oriented being. He loves mathematics, he even gave them to us so that we could better understand his creation. It is part of who God is.

I've had this book called Biblical Mathematics by Evangelist Ed F. Vallowe, for a very long time. This book delves deeply into the numbers within God's creation. Where I might skim over, give highlights and general meanings, Vallowe provides the in-depth definitions for numerical significance. More importantly, I've learned the relationship numbers have to the Hebraic alphabet. Jews actually use numbers in certain mathematical formulas, called gematria. It is believed among certain Jewish scholars that gematria denotes secrets of the Torah. If you really want to get into all of the depth of a numeric repetition, and how it's tied into the Scripture, use your concordance. It will tell you how many times a word is in the Bible. It'll tell you how many times a number is in the Bible, and what those numbers mean.

CYCLES CARRY SIGNIFICANCE

There are just certain cycles of day that carry significance in the spirit realm. As an intercessor for example, I don't have to glance at a clock to know when it's four o'clock. It doesn't matter what season I'm in, or even which time zone. I can see natural and spiritual indicators that let me know it's four o'clock. We are able to grow accustomed to a time where our spirit is acutely alert. Our physical body is able to acclimate to what our spirit prioritizes. Just like you have your internal alarm. You know when it's time to get up or eat a meal, and it's not just because of your habits, not always, at least.

Significant cycles vary from person to person to a certain extent. Some people wake up at three o'clock every morning. That's because their spirit is sensing a shift. That is a time to conquer and wage spiritual warfare. It's a time God is calling his people into intercession. These times are sacred. Your spirit will tell your body the times that are significant, when it needs to be on high alert, or when to rest.

Cycles are sacred. We already know that days are sacred such as the Sabbath which begins on Friday's sunset. However a larger form of time that carries equal significance happens through the cycle of months.

Each month actually starts not with a full moon, but when there is nothing but a little sliver of moon. Sometimes when there was substantial cloud cover, the representatives for each tribe were spread out to have the greatest vantage point to see the moon. The moon determined when the new month began so accuracy was vitally important. Numerous witnessed reports were required for the sake of accuracy. They watched for the times and seasons. Times have been appointed by God and he desires that we recognize changes in them when they occur.

When the tribes saw the new moon, it signaled the new month—the head of the month. It's considered the first fruits. It's a time of celebration and honor. I've seen this done both ways. I've seen people pay their first fruits at the front of the Gregorian calendar month and others give their first fruits at the head of the Hebraic. I'm not going to tell you one is right, or one is wrong. God will honor you for giving your first fruits. That's where I'm going to stand. Test it if you're not sure. Put your first fruits where you feel you're led because God is faithful to prove his loving kindnesses by honoring his word.

Our new week begins on the Gregorian Sunday. The month gets a little complicated because the Hebraic month they go 29 to 30 days instead of 30 to 31. Instead of having a leap day once every four years, their calendar is actually broken into 19-year segments. Certain years are marked and assigned to be leap years even if they're forty years down the road. What happens in the leap year is you have a 13-day month called Adar the second or Adar II. This leap month is associated with the tribe of Levi. But remember, in the Hebraic calendar, the seventh year is a year of Jubilee. A year of celebration where all debts are cancelled. Jubilee!

There's not a lot of harvest that year, because everything is supposed to rest in the year of jubilee. Our God honors that year. It's a season for everything to rest; everything to be forgiven because it's a sign of what God's doing through his Son and it's that gift of rest he's offered us. A Hebraic Jubilee year was 5777. It just so happened that was the same time as the 70th anniversary of Israel. Seventy also represents jubilee because it's a 'seven' year. Seven is the number of completion in the Bible.

The Hebraic head of the year is like our January, except it occurs in Fall known as the month of Tishri. Since it's the head of the year, it's also a first fruit for the new year—like our January occurring around the Winter solstice.

God's head of the year is in the Fall. The month of Tishri was the first month under the tribe of Reuben who was the firstborn. But in Exodus 12 we read, "The Lord said to Moses, and Aaron in Egypt, 'this month is to be for you the first month, the first month of your year.'" He's not saying this is the first month of the new year, he's not talking about the new year at all, actually, but this is the ordained first month of the year. *Not Tishri where I have you now. I'm moving this and this is going to be the Passover. Tell the whole community of Israel, that on the 10th day of this month, each man is to take the lamb for his family, one of each household.* Then He goes on to describe what they're supposed to do with this lamb. And if they don't have enough in their household for a whole lamb, what they're supposed to do, come together, and they take the blood. They're having the Passover and they take the blood from that lamb, and they put it on their door posts. It resembles a letter in the Hebraic alphabet.

They put it on the doorpost and what happens? When the plague of death sweeps through Egypt, they are spared the fate of whoever did not have the blood on the doorpost; not only is their firstborn son taken, but everything that they own that is firstborn: livestock, slaves or otherwise. Every firstborn died that wasn't marked by the blood over the door because it had not come out of the curse of death in the land.

God established his Passover right there. He said, *Because of the Passover, because you have allowed the blood to cover you and your first gifts, your first fruits, I am going to mark this time*. Not only does this become a high holy fast period in the year, but it also become the first month of the year.

The calendar changes. It moves from Tishri, which is now the seventh month of the year, to the seventh month, which is now the first month, which is Nisan through March and April. After that comes Iyar and all the rest. What happened is the Head of the Year is still in Tishri because he's still honoring the first fruit of Jacob, but the Head of Months now falls in Nisan. Now those months become a double first fruit. It's a representation of the Passover, Jesus' blood. It's the representation of all the first fruits that God gave to Israel. I will note that in Exodus 12 the law had not been given yet, so the Passover was established before the law. This was what we call the precepts of God because it was established without the law. The Passover, just like the seventh day, Nisan and the Year of jubilee, carries significance for more than just being particular time in the year.

Passover is a precept like the first fruits. When God said take Isaac up to the mountain to sacrifice him there, God was asking for the first fruits through Isaac. Abraham was willing to sacrifice Isaac in obedience to God. However an angel interrupted by providing another sacrifice. The angel told Abraham God was going to use Isaac to bring the Messiah. The offering of the first fruits and firstborn is a precept of God.

The Passover is a big deal to God, that's why it's one of the high holy days, but the fact that it was established before the law means that it has relevance today. Does that mean that you need to paint animal blood on your doorposts? No, but we do have to pay attention to it because of what we know of appointed times and seasons. We can't just discard it because it's Old Testament. It will have validity when Jesus reigns in the New Jerusalem; I can guarantee you we're going to celebrate Passover with Jesus. Whether you do now or not, and whether you observe the high holy days, fasts and feast is ultimately between you and God.

CHARACTERISTICS OF THE MONTHS

There are certain characteristics that accompany each particular month, and these are lined up with the 12 tribes of Israel. We covered the days, the twelve-hour markers, the week, where the Sabbath falls and where that new week begins. We talked about the month being 29 to 30 days as opposed to 30 or 31 and the new moon. We've talked about the year and how the head of the year is still in Tishri, but the head of the month is in Nisan, which is in spring. God had seasons begin in Fall and the Spring, not Winter and Summer. Remember sunset - Fall. Then Winter, the dark night, when we're sleeping and resting. Then we spring up from our rest with the sunrise, which is the beginning of the new month.

There is a tribe for every month, each tribe represents one of the sons of Israel. They have their color stone and their birthstone just like we do with the Gregorian. There is a Hebrew letter that corresponds to a particular tribe and month. Every letter also represents a picture, but not always in the way you may think. You're going oh, that's the constellation Pisces so that's going to represent the fish. No. The meanings are all inter-woven like a braided cord threaded throughout the entire year. Then all re-cycles again. The focus is to bring us back to our intentional purposes through the redemption of Jesus Christ.

Sometimes we can be out swimming at the beach only to find ourselves caught in a riptide. A riptide has the ability to carry us farther out of our intentional path. Before too long, you don't even realize where you are anymore. You try to swim back to the shore. When you feel exhausted, and it seems you're getting nowhere, not knowing why; it could be because you're swimming against the riptide. When you recognize you are in a riptide, swim with a riptide so you actually move yourself out of the riptide. Sometimes, we need to get our bearings about us to reposition for a disposition.

Our year is all about getting your emotions intact and each month has its own intentional focus. If I am unable to bring my emotions in alignment when I go through something, it may hold me back in the next month or the progression of the year. Unattended emotions can grow into something like a grudge. If we allow that 'grudge' to continue without confronting it, then we are participating in sin. Why? Because we are to align ourselves back into the alignment of God. We are offended when he is offended. We forgive as God forgives. We confront as he confronts. Evaluating our mindful disposition strengthens us in a way that we die to self, producing more of harvest in the nature of God.

Have you heard me talk about going into a certain land where all of a sudden one of your spiritual or redemptive gifts is going through the roof? *I don't do this at home, what's going on?* There's a gifting on that land that you've just stepped into. Now it's flowing out of you because you're on the land. The same is true when you step into the identity of a particular month and you understand what it is, what it means.

There are certain keys that will unlock things that have been guarded from you but when you acknowledge that they're there, you can simply unlock it through your obedience and through your worship. Now you can receive the fullness of it and totally start changing the purpose that you're in. It's just powerful stuff. These cycles through time that are in the land either assist us or hinder us in our effectiveness in our purpose depending on whether we are moving in the spirit of light or darkness. You determine how they are supposed to operate through the practice of righteous discipline.

When we understand how God's times and season work, then we can begin to understand when he's changing the times and seasons in our purpose. He'll begin to give us things like dreams, or words, or somebody will start feeling uncomfortable, or something will feel detached. Perhaps something will just pull out of you; this, longing that pulls you toward it. Like, *I just have to get there. I don't know what it is, but I have to go. I don't know why. I don't know what's waiting for me on the other side, but I know I'm supposed to be there. I've got to do it and I have to do it now.* That's when you recognize that the purpose, the times and seasons are shifting. He will give us the signs if we search for them.

The Seed, Sower, and Reaper came as promised through Abraham. Jesus came through the lineage of Isaac. The Antichrist comes from the seed of Ishmael. We don't really hear a lot about Abraham's other children, but when Sarah died, Abraham remarried. There are a few verses on that and that's about all you see. Those children who followed did not receive an inheritance. They didn't receive the blessing; they received a portion.

Do you recall when Joseph said, *We are going to eat from this portion and put some back, because we're not in the famine?* Abraham was setting a certain portion of his own provision back for these

Ancestral Purpose

children. He did not use what was the birthright of Isaac or of Isaac's blessing. Everything that he had first went to Isaac. Everything Abraham had after that went to his other children. He had already given Ishmael a blessing when Abaraham sent him away some years earlier.

There is a time to set back a portion, another to be the provision of the birthright and yet another as the blessing. This is a kingdom principle that we typically associate to giving, but it is a kingdom principle of inheritance. This is legacy.

Everything was lined up to go to Isaac, but Abraham had been setting some back of his personal portion for the children of Katurah. They didn't receive the blessing and they didn't receive any birthright, of course.

This was something Abraham understood when he saw Melchizedek. When Abraham gave his tithes to Melchizedek, God immediately blesses Abraham with a covenant blessing. Isaac was the promise, the first fruits of that covenant. Isaac, not Ishmael, because God said, "You and Sarah." Hagar wasn't even really in the picture. She was not in the forefront. She was only in the forefront when their fear and anxiety started manifesting. Their fear and anxiety, their doubt and unbelief were canceling out the promise of God. It was denying His power, denying His authority. That's why Ishmael doesn't represent the covenant of God although God did bless Ishmael. Jesus was the fulfillment of the first fruits offering of God which fulfilled the covenant through Abraham. Now through the covenant of God fulfilled through Jesus, we are able to join in God's original intent of order in the earth, separating ourselves from darkness and into His marvelous light.

A few chapters ahead, you will begin to study Times and Seasons of God. You will see into the twelve tribes of Israel but as you review them, consider how they are the first government of God in the earth until Jesus. Then as Jesus as an innocent sacrifice and resurrection restored the Sons of God in the earth through the body of believers. They knew the King of Kings had come to the earth, but as he prepares a place for us even now, the ecclesia is responsible for preparing his bride in the earth.

Throughout time God has used patterns. His scriptures are full of them. Yahweh set the universe in its formation, and it obeys through the synchronization of time. Even over two thousand years ago, a single star declared the wonder of the Lord's majesty. The Messiah had come.

We need to know how to understand God's message in his patterns. As you read through this book about purpose, I will be doing my best to show you how the old and new testaments overlay. You can pass through life without knowing this information, but I sincerely believe that your life cycles will become abundantly clearer when you utilize God's patterns throughout.

Just as there are four seasons in the year, each one has a pattern for the sowing and the reaping. When considering the growth of a tree, or the function of a human body, there is known to be a seen aspect and an unseen aspect. So it is with the spiritual things. As you grow internally, changes occur internally to support that growth.

Four key elements are used when teaching the Hebraic patterns found in the cycle of the year through the months: 1) Tribes of Israel, 2) Constellation of the Stars, 3) Letters of the Hebraic Alphabet, and 4) Seasons.

Other patterns in God's purposes are the feasts and fasts of the High Holy days, first fruits, gematria in numbers, stones of the tribes, and prayer watches. Use your study guide to connect it all together.

We are designed to prosper in the provision of God's covenant so long as we stay aligned in his times and seasons. Stay with me through this journey and you will see how to insert the implementation of these valuable tools. When we seed healthily, we reap healthily.

5

PURPOSE OF ECCLESIA

As we finish up purpose, we're going to see how God has taken us through this journey of purpose to reveal not only what our purpose is, but how we exercise it with authority in the earth. God is an expert painter, and every stroke has a place in the masterpiece. It's astounding to me what he's putting together even now. We know our identity, we're coming in tune with our purpose, we're walking it out and now we just need to take this show on the road. It is a truly unique gift that we get to make this journey together.

BRIDE OF PURPOSE

God's purpose is our purpose. This will always remain the main thing as we live our life. We've learned that when we understand our identity through our purpose and the common thread that connects everything we've done since the beginning, it takes us to new experiences in changing times and seasons. My focus today may appear different than it will five years from now, but it still has that same common thread—whether that's a skill, personality trait or something else. When you look back, even on a resume, you can find certain things that identify your connecting feature. Then you ask yourself what about that links me to my purpose? It doesn't matter if you are an artistic person who can think through abstract dimension and pull things in from different areas to make something become a beautiful bouquet of glory, or whether you're a linear processor who sees things as an exact science which brings stability through order. God made us all with different proficiencies and personalities that connect us to our purpose.

I once heard somebody explain the differences between a mathematician and an engineer. With a mathematician, everything is an exact science; you're looking for a specific answer to every problem. However, in engineering, you're just looking for an answer to a specific situation. You're looking for the solution, but it only has to be right enough to provide the solution necessary to get from point A to point B. Even though the two seem similar, each one working their course through an equation, the way they get to their solution is vastly different.

The same is true with purpose. Even though I am in the body of believers of the Messiah, when Jesus becomes your Messiah, you are also part of that body—we all make up its composition. What I do is going to be different from what Jacob does, which is different from what Lola does. We are all specifically unique and different. I can meet somebody who shares my redemptive gift, but they may be operating on totally different strengths and talents than I have. Their process is different, but yet we have similarities. It's not just the bond of being the body of Christ, it's also the bond that we are working to accomplish the same goal.

Space engineers work to build the most advanced and durable spaceship they can create, and the mathematicians are diligently working to figure out what they have to do to get that spaceship to come through the atmosphere at the right time to avoid exploding. They're both working towards the same goal, they're just working at separate angles on the same project. That's what I'm talking about when I say, "Stay in your lane". If you're a mathematician, stay in your lane. If you're an engineer, stay in your lane; know your purpose, and know how you're going to get to your destiny. Each person is still unique with their own process in God's purpose. How they do it and get there is between them and God.

If I swerve into Louis' lane and do his job for him, who will be doing the task I am assigned? Louis and I both need to stay in our lane, and Louis needs to understand his identity and be sure-footed in his purpose so somebody can't come alongside him and say, *Louis, I know you keep calling yourself an engineer, but you're really a mathematician.* He needs to be able to say, *No, I'm an engineer, and you can't tell me otherwise.* Our gifts and God's call upon us are absolutely irrevocable according to Romans 11:29.

Ancestral Purpose

We have to understand how we're going to approach those situations so that we can't be shaken off our base or moved into a different lane. I tried to operate out of the wrong lane for a long time. It didn't work out very well. It led to frustration, meltdowns and passionate expressions that were not always healthy. I was trying to be something that I was not rather than accepting who I was. Now I can reflect back and say, *Wow, I was trying to operate in my authority when I didn't understand my identity or my purpose.* I like to think of it like Lincoln Logs. My purpose needs to be stacked up between my identity and authority, the pieces locking together, just like our DNA code. I've tried for years to walk in my authority when I didn't have a good understanding of who I was. And since I didn't know who I was, it made it even harder for me to understand who God was. I was seeing through a damaged filter. It's a two-way relationship. I wasn't able to fully step into the understanding of him, and I didn't understand that I was really grasping at straws. I didn't have a clue because people were telling me I was this, or I was supposed to be like this, and these people were saying will you just pick something?

I got to the point where I just threw everything out and said, *Okay God, who do you say I am?* Then my understanding of who I was according to God began to come into focus. God began to come into focus as well. When I could see me through his eyes, it automatically brought me closer to him. I could suddenly get close enough to see his face. I could get so close that I could smell him like the summer rain accented by the fragrance of flowers in full bloom. I could feel his glory around me; it was tangible. And I learned how to embrace him. The closer I got to him, the more he came into focus, and the more he came into focus, the more I could see my reflection in his eyes. I could see the things that I needed to expand on. Yet I could see the things that I needed to shut down completely. I turned from wicked ways and false identities that either established stumbling blocks or baggage through life's journey. Those things didn't belong to me because God had a separate identity in store for me. I just couldn't see it. I had this filter on called 'experience' and it altered my reflection. It was necessary

Purpose of Ecclesia

to change lenses. His lenses are pure and reflect a lot of light making the ability to see much easier.

So now we know that for those who love God, all things work together for good. The birthright, the blessing, the livelihood, time management and our health, all the things that consume our every day, family, business, our favor, our property, they all work together for our good. Why? Because when we love God, our filters start coming off so we can see who he really is. When I did this, I began to understand the heart of God, and the more I learned about him, the more I was learning about myself. The more I purged ungodliness within myself, the closer I came to him. I got so close that people I knew for fifteen years no longer recognized me. I appeared the same physically, but the Spirit within me was completely different. It changed my identity, and the blood of Jesus has come and washed the old things away so that his glory could fill me. And now they're beginning to see the glory of God permeate beyond my identity.

This becomes our purpose: for our life to reveal Jesus to others. That moves people into questions, into conviction and wanting change in their own lives. Most people want to share their story with me, no matter where I am; they're compelled to share their heart with me. Why? Because they're encountering the glory, not Rebecca. I'm here today, gone tomorrow, but God's love is eternal and will open every door. That is what people are to see.

For those who are called according to his purpose. All things work together for the good of those who are called. If you love God, you are called according to his purposes. That means whatever time he has for you, in whatever season, you are to fulfill his purposes to best of your ability. It is within him. I do not work independently of God, but I work whenever and wherever he tells me.

I am married to my husband, Crispin, but I am not attached to him at the hip. I can wake up an hour later than he does. I can take my shower and eat what I want for breakfast. I can let my personality come through and he can allow his personality to come through, but yet, we are still one. God didn't ask you to change who he created you to be, he's asking you to be that person he created and loves beyond compare. Whether you're quiet or loud, assertive or passive, he designed you the way that you are so that you could accomplish his purposes in the earth. I love my husband, but I can't work his job for him. God created him for a specific side of a specific purpose, and I would be doing both of us a disservice if I tried to come in and be Crispin.

OUR BIRTHRIGHT IN CHRIST

Mark 16:15, Jesus tells his disciples, "Go into all the world and preach the good news to all creation."

That's a pretty clear message, right? We are to go into the earth and teach the good news of Jesus Christ because he is our deliverer, and everything about God was done around his son. We talked about the constellations and how they were a witness of the coming Messiah. Even in The Old Testament, everything was leading up to Jesus. That's how we're supposed to be so that everyone sees Christ through us. He's given us the authority—that's the one thing that should demonstrate Christ more than anything, and that only requires us to stay in our lane and do what we've been called to do. No matter how it seems. No matter if that's singing, praying, fasting or whatever he has you doing at the moment, we do what we've been called to do, just like Jesus.

Because we are walking in our identity, we understand our birthright. This is important. We talked about the transformation that took place in our identity through Christ Jesus. As such, we then learned to walk out our salvation through the understanding that we now have a birth right in Christ Jesus. Through our obedience to Christ we receive the blessings of Father's abundance.

When Isaac was born, he had his father's birthright. But when Abraham died, God came and blessed Isaac in Genesis 25. Abraham gave his birthright to Isaac, not to the other sons. He had another wife, but he only gave those sons gifts, things he had set aside, but not what belonged to Isaac. We all have access to that birthright.

Another example is the sons of Gideon: seventy legitimate sons and one illegitimate. And then suddenly, all seventy were living out that birthright with their father, not just one, all of them. Can you imagine? Sharing a kingdom with seventy sons.

So we have that birthright, and when we walk in our identity, the blessing comes through the Father. It comes through that worship of obedience. When we receive grace freely, that's our birthright. We didn't do anything to earn it, but because we were born again, we received grace. When we share that grace, that adoption, and we take the time to pray with someone in need, when we don't show anger when someone wrongs us, if we show love, then God is able to move through that situation and heal that person. When our grace is given, God comes and pours his greater grace out on the situation. So I am blessed, they are blessed, and the situation is blessed.

God loves it when we demonstrate his heart to others. He basically says, *You are your brother's keeper. It is your responsibility. I didn't leave you to the wilderness to die. I brought you all the way, I'm growing you here for something better. I brought you here for my covenant. I want to give it to you, but you have to walk in your purpose and identity.* God is saying that he won't walk into the promised land for you.

You have to pick your feet up and march another five miles. He'll be right beside you the whole time, but you have to do the labor. When you get there, his promises will be supplied. You will see God's covenant released to you, just as he told your forefathers. When we do that, there is no other choice. It defies all earthly law because it's God's law, which takes precedence over everything. But science always falls into God's law. Miracles, signs and wonders have to follow us—it's in the Word. They have to because we carry the glory of God, and Jesus Christ sent his Spirit to fill us. It's not about our mind or power, it is by his Spirit. We just have to be willing to walk that out in our times and seasons, understanding who we are, that we carry the mantle of authority, and that he's given us the keys to the kingdom. We don't have to raise a hand. We don't have to say a word. We can walk through a department store and people will be slain in the spirit and have encounters with God.

They can be convicted and won over to redemption. Walk in the authority the LORD has given us.

I am ready to see more of God's glory released. I am ready to see the transformation of the kingdom. I'm ready to see his kingdom at hand. I'm ready to see my savior return. I am ready to see people's hearts undone. I am ready to see it all. First we have to be the ecclesia. You and I will have to take an active role in God's kingdom; we have to take those steps into the promised land. We can't cut a corner on the sixth day. We have to go all the way around the wall that seventh time to witness the victory of the Lord. And we have to bring the restoration that God has appointed for this season.

FATHER'S AUTHORITY

Being a spectator is not good enough. Gideon was the only one out of his clan that arose to defy the enemy. He had an army, but God kept cutting the number down until there were only three hundred men to be used. What if it only took three hundred men's determination? Could God do it with just five? Of course he could: he's God, he doesn't need us, but he loves us enough to let us be part of his plans. We're in covenant relationship with him, and that means something to him. When God's glory cloud moves, we move with him. We don't just stand on the sidelines; he wants us to move with his power. He desires us to move with his glory. He wishes us to be an expression of himself on Earth.

Why has the Ark of the Covenant been hidden so long? Because WE are supposed to carry the glory. Authority is permission to act without permission. Claudette has a certain authority to make certain purchases, without having to go and ask every five seconds. There are certain expenditures that are in her area that she has approval make. When it comes to her personal finances, she has 100% authority, but in her job, she only has a measure of authority. If she needs to step beyond her authority, she has to go to someone who has more authority than herself.

Sometimes we have to go to the Father to get permission for more authority. People say, *Oh, it is freely given, blah, blah, blah.* Let's go back to the core value of honor begetting honor. Yes, it is freely given, but I need to make sure that Father has qualified my ability to foster such a responsibility. I can't come into the city like a storm and declare that I have authority to take this town especially if I've not stewarded the last city. You know what will happen? I'll be laughed right back out of town—and never mind the spiritual warfare I'll encounter. I have to be honorable. I'm coming into foreign land, right? So we start relationship by relationship.

Going into new territory is what God has called me to do. I want to share my heart and let you know that I'm praying for your city, your county, your ministry. I'm praying that God's purposes come to order in your territory. I'm praying and sharing my heart because that builds relationship, it establishes honor.

I once had somebody ask for prayer over their property. This was great. The only catch was that she did not have permission from her spouse. When I heard about that, I said, *No. I'm sorry, I would love to come pray, but without approval, we cannot come. It is dishonorable.* Remember, honor begets honor. *What if we just don't tell him?* Wait a minute; we do not operate out of deceit. If I can't walk in spiritual integrity, how is this woman's spouse going to see Jesus? The man is still head of household and is to be respected; though husband and wife are co-leaders, the husband is ultimately the priest of his home, even when he's not living righteously.

So we prayed for God's strategies from afar, and God completely delivered. That strategy actually had to do with things in and around the one who wanted us to come. Once we started praying that strategy, things changed. The woman's husband was healed, chaos and confusion dissipated, restoration manifested, and relationships started healing. Even though honor wasn't necessarily deserved in this situation, we honored this woman's husband and like God was saying, *Because you've been steady and faithful to seek my face, I'm going to remember that grace.*

When we honor others, God returns honor to us with a portion greater than the original. The entire household changed because of our prayer and honor, becoming a place of rest and hope again. We can be effective in warfare even while maintaining distance. You don't win by disrespecting the home; you might lose that man forever. The goal is to have him find Christ through honor or miracles, or whatever means God uses. God's ways are greater than ours. He knows the situation from the beginning to its end. We may have a ton of knowledge, but when we trust him to direct our paths, he will meet us there and fulfill his purposes. As long as we're Kingdom minded, he will bring the transformation required to produce miracles, signs and wonders.

We have the authority to bring Heaven to earth, but we must remember that authority originates with God, and he delegates it to us through our relationship with his son.

PURPOSE IN ACTION
We don't have to test God; all we need to do is be obedient and make sure that everything we do and say is done in love and honor. In Matthew 10, Jesus called his twelve disciples to himself and gave them authority to drive out evil spirits and to heal every disease. That is our birthright. When you understand your identity and purpose, you know that seeing and doing these things will become a common theme throughout your life. Even though the times and seasons may have you presented in a different way, the core is the same. Your redemptive gift will mature. Your fivefold gift may become more pronounced, but only because it's beginning to deepen. You can now walk in that gift confidently knowing that it's yours.

Jesus called us to drive out evil spirits. Some believers think, *Oh, no. We don't see that very often.* Well, have you ever wondered why the land is so wicked? Now, granted, I don't just go into New Orleans and knock out every evil spirit, that would be foolish, even dishonorable. I need to know my assignment before going in, and I also need to ask the Father how I'm supposed to act in that situation. *How do you want me to do this here?*

Here's an example: If Veronica goes fishing and she's never fished a day in her life, and I don't tell her how to fish, her chances of landing a ten-pound bass are going to be pretty slim. I have to say, *Okay, here's how we do this.* I have to go through the list to explain what tackle to use and how to bait the hook—I may even need to show her how to catch a fish. Sometimes we have to ask God what our purpose does in action. Sometimes we have to say, *Lord, you said you wanted me to fast, but what would you like me to fast and for how long?* Take the time to ask God exactly what he wants. We accept the call to fast, but immediately choose something that's tolerable for our flesh. I don't mind going without caffeine, but Lord help me if you take away my chocolate. I think I'll go without the caffeine. Does this sound familiar?

We need to be intentional about our fasting because God is going to be intentional about meeting us in that place. We are fasting for a purpose. We are fasting to see results. We are fasting because there are times you're going to have to fast and pray to draw out certain spirits. I can't just walk up and say, *Hit the road, buddy.* That work for some, but not for all. I have to know the assignment and the appointed time. I have to walk in my purpose during the appropriate season knowing that it has been established. It doesn't happen like that every time, but it often does. Two people manifested demonic spirits in front of me just recently; it happens. We need to be on guard and ready to do battle wherever the Spirit of the Lord calls us.

The gospel that Jesus preached is our purpose; the lifestyle of discipleship and miracles is to be a model for our lives. But we must be careful that we don't get so caught up in the gifts and the purpose that we fail to seek his will on how to use them. A purpose without a plan is a gun without a target. It is through our diligent seeking of God's face and sitting at his feet that we learn how our purpose is to be used. The Kingdom thrives when populated by a people that earnestly seek the King.

HIS WILL, NOT OURS

The kingdom of heaven is near. This is the gospel we are to preach. We can speak of God's love and kindness. We are privileged to tell people the joyous news of his love for them, and how he desires to set them free from affliction. He wants to heal them. He wants to break curses off their lives. But while we preach the gospel, heal the sick, raise the dead and cleanse the lepers, we have to be mindful that we tell people how much God loves them. When I went to Spain, this was the Scripture I hung onto. I was angry at God. *You said that we could heal the sick and raise the dead,* I shouted at him. He calmly replied, *Are you asking me what I want you to do? I want to demonstrate my love, but are you telling people about it?*

I was asking for the right thing—a scriptural thing—but for all the wrong reasons. My flesh was definitely involved; I had a little pride rise up in me. Jesus said that we could raise the dead and heal the sick, so we're just going to pray and it's going to be done, right? Well, here's the thing, our motives play a significant role in seeing those things manifest, and it just so happens that my motives were not entirely true. I was pondering what I could do to help God, and not asking God how he wanted to use me.

He may have wanted me to fast and pray. He may have wanted me to give up a few weeks of my life to seek him in prayer. But I never took the time to ask him. I didn't understand my authority in the right regard. I wasn't honoring the Father; I was taking it upon myself to make things happen. I put his signet ring on my finger, and I was willing to set things in order, I just didn't ask for direction first. I was playing games with God's authority. I was playing dress up, and I still didn't understand my identity. I was still grappling with who I was in Jesus Christ, but yet I was making demands of him to show up and be God for me. It sounds absurd, but my heart was never in the wrong place. There may have been a little personal intent behind there, but I didn't see it at the time, I just wanted to see the Kingdom established wherever I was.

I was seeing God through a filter based on how I wanted to see him. Now that I seek his will first, I can understand my identity and operate strategically in prayer and warfare. It is a desire of my heart to see lepers cleansed, demons drawn out and the kingdom of God established on earth. I am seeing these things more and more as I seek him. Freely I have received grace, and freely I will give it to others. We have to demonstrate his grace. We have to be more loving, more kind, patient and long suffering. Every time I show grace, I get to see a new dimension of God. I get to see him a little deeper than I did yesterday. I get to see more of this face, and the deeper we go in his glory, the less we are looking at his hands, because it becomes about his face. Yes, it is okay to see his hands, but his face reveals our destiny.

When we were writing our prayers for the song, and writing for the ministry, I took a piece of paper and also wrote a prayer for my business. As we worked our way through Nissan, I prayed those prayers every day. When we got all the way through, I scanned the prayers and thought, *These don't necessarily sound like God's plans.* My thoughts were wrapped up in personal things like how much I'd like to have a truck to haul stuff around. Even believing, that truck was nowhere in sight. Nowhere. We're all human, right? Reflecting a minute, I laid my heart before the Lord, and realized that my true desire was not for personal possessions, my heart was sincere after the things of God and his kingdom.

Everything in my life is to reflect that. Shortly, the prayers were revised to reflect his heart. I prayed into them all the harder. There was not a personal want in there. Even though some of the things had to do with my personal business or our ministry, there was not a personal intention for my gain anywhere in there. And just a few days after the month of Nissan, I was already feeling the spiritual synergy of the kingdom of God behind those prayers. I still do. And there were some things I didn't even ask for that you'd think I would. I didn't ask God to protect or love my kids; I already know that he promises to take care of them. I don't have to seek his hand for things he's already promised. He knows my thoughts before I even ask him anything. If it's truly a need, he will know, but I don't have any needs because I know he is faithful to supply everything. And even if I did, I revert to the covenant. I know that God has the cattle on a thousand hills. I know he's given me joy. My healing of deliverance is complete. I have no death in me, I only have life because of who Jesus is. Everything I might possibly need; he has already provided. I don't need to search his hands anymore; I can gaze at his face. I can consult him in everything. *Hey, Papa, did you* see in the newspaper that this thing came up? What would you like us to do about that? Is this something that we take now, or should we put this on the back burner? Do you have something in mind? These are the kind of conversations I have with my God. Circumstances around us are temporal but we need to know how we utilize them to produce change. What needs to be considered is how to bring his kingdom here, on earth as it is in Heaven. He has a plan. We partner with him to complete it. This is Kingdom.

USING OUR AUTHORITY

Completion is here, but we have to tap into it. It's a choice, and our choices make a difference and affect others. I can choose to sit down and not let my glory show. Have you ever done that? I certainly have. I'll have days where I just do not want to be bothered with anything. I love people, but not all the time. Sometimes I just need to be alone. When we were in transition, I remember going into churches, and I would literally put my coat on before I stepped in the church. I did not want to be seen or heard. I did not want to share any of the light and life that was within me. I could do that because even though it's God's glory, he's placed it within me. We have the right to keep our light under a bushel. When you are in an uncomfortable situation, you can take your spiritual cloak and become invisible. This is not operating out of a demonic spirit, it is a privilege and a right that you have as an heir with Christ, to be by yourself, because sometimes you need to be. You can't always be on fire. There are times where you need to retreat. There are times where Crispin, as much as he's a people lover, has to take a step back—though he usually takes me with him. It's not misuse of the glory; it's just taking care of yourself.

I was in New Orleans recently and I heard a strange noise outside the place I was staying. I recognized it as a dog, but there was something not quite right about it. So there was already a commotion, but then I kept hearing this screeching crow. *What is a crow doing here?* I wondered. So I went outside, and stared at the crow like, "What are you doing? Why are you making these terrible noises? Just shut up."

Purpose of Ecclesia

It became so bad that I finally decided, *Okay, I'm going to sing.* The moment I did, the crow would shut up, but the dog would start barking instead. Nothing was helping and I had no idea what to do about it. I asked God and he said, 'By your spirit command that crow to shove off; show it whose spirit lives inside of you.' That's when it started to click for me. Once my spirit came forward, I told that crow to go. You know what? That crow turned his head toward me before it flew off. When the crow flew off, the dog got quiet too.

I did what the father told me to do. I knew that there was something going on. I didn't know why that crow was there, but it was creating such a disturbance that I could hear it above everything else going on. It was just trying to be a distraction. Isn't that just like the enemy to try to distract us or irritate us? When the singing didn't help, that's where I dug my heels in. My spiritual sound has authority over the enemy. Father didn't offer to tell me what to do until I asked. His advice didn't require me to understand the legality of his instructions, but only to obey. He, being a good father, walked me through it. Guess what? It worked.

God used that moment as training for me. If I hadn't honored by taking the time to hear him, I would have missed it, and that crow would have been there as a resounding symbol all night long. It only took two seconds to ask; *What do you want me to do?* Honor begets honor. We have the ability, authority, and permission to act, but there are times to ask for more authority. This allows us to step into more authority. By recognizing that we, in ourselves, are not enough. By taking time to ask God first, we demonstrate humility and honor. Success in the assignment is when we demonstrate maturity by acknowledging we are not enough to handle the assignment by ourselves.

THE FIRST ECCLESIA

The twelve tribes of the nation of Israel were created from the covenant of God through Abraham and his descendants. This was God's establishment on the earth after Adam. The Law was given through the two tablets Moses brought down from the mountain.

Kings were placed over the nation because the people wanted a king. God desired that they would honor him as king. There was a government established in the earth according to God's precepts. The problem was that they lacked relationship with God. The law was meant to bring them together, but because they were separated from God and wanted their own way there was little to no honor of God at all. Therefore, without relationship, the kingdom of God could not be balanced in revelation and understanding. The government of God became a destructive tool in the hands of the people.

THE SECOND ECCLESIA

Jesus, the very seed of God, came to restore the government of god through relationship. Jesus did as his father instructed him to do in the character and likeness of his Father. This restored the righteous government of God's kingdom in the earth. Through relationships whereby we honor one another as ourselves and give God first place in our lives through a lifetime of servitude, we restore God's kingdom on earth.

The gift of Holy Spirit, given by Jesus, directs us according to Father's desires, to mature in righteousness in every aspect of life. Sowing righteous seeds produces more of the righteousness of God. Therefore, walking uprightly in our understanding of purpose produces discipleship in others through various seasons of sonship. This process is a physical manifestation to what has occurred spiritually within us. Everything that happens in Spirit must manifest in the earth. Happenings in the physical will manifest something of spirit: light or darkness, life or death.

Without us demonstrating the Kingdom of God in the earth, the darkness cannot be penetrated. The New Testament is our example to live by. The Old Testament serves as a historical reminder for mistakes that need not reoccur and covenants providing restoration. It is the ecclesia who bring accountability to the people of the world and enforce disciplines that produce change through miracles, signs, and wonders. No one knows a man's heart but Father. We do not judge a man's heart, but we can see his heart

Purpose of Ecclesia

by the fruit he produces. The fruit of the government of God through the ecclesia is rooted in love. Love breaks the chains of bondage. Love restores freedom and liberty. Love pierces the darkness because God is love.

LIFE IN PURPOSE

As the ecclesia, it is God's heart that we connect with one another on a spiritual level to achieve his heart. It is important that we are able to identify one another and create a sense of family community like the tribes of Israel and the disciples. We are to be like-minded. That doesn't mean we are supposed to be programmed robots but to be ourselves in this journey we call life. We are to understand who we are, why we are, to do what God has called us to do.

The courage and determination it takes to stay within community is to be celebrated. It does take discipline and humility. When you find your community, just know in advance that it will be flawed. Afterall, people are involved. Already determine in your heart to forgive them before any transgression occurs so you can address it according to scripture while keeping your hand steady to the work of the kingdom. Likewise, you may make mistakes also. Yep, you. Be open to receive correction so you may mature in longsuffering and humility. Be ready to repent and forgive. No man is an island, no should he be. C'mon. Let's do life together as the ecclesia in the Kingdom of Go

6

TIMES & SEASONS

Times and seasons matter. They are meant to be identifiers of change(s) needing to transpire within ourselves. These changes are for the benefit of promoting growth, development, and health in conjunction with God's order. Recognizing the change in times and seasons is for the purpose of establishing maturity for the next move God has planned for his people. Isaiah 46:10 says that God makes known the end from the beginning and from the ancient times, he knows what is still to come. He continues to say that his purpose will stand, and he will do as he pleases. In other words, he has a plan and will complete it. His intentionality directs us to follow that purpose through the times and seasons. The more we walk in our purpose in agreement with his intention according to his pattern in each new season and time, we come closer to fulfilling our destiny.

TIMES

An aspect of time is a longer duration of time that is more linear than circular. In order to make a visual distinction, consider the circle versus a figure eight. The infinity sign of a figure eight represents time. A time is something that will not be again within the time continuum that God created for the establishment of his Kingdom. A given time has a beginning and an end, but it doesn't repeat like a cycle of time will.

A person's life is a time. An age is a time. The Renaissance Age is a time. Throughout time are different aspects of time that mark singular events that will not repeat. Wars represent times. Some wars are centuries long and other wars are short, but no two are alike. The objectives and outcomes are typically the same, but no one war is the same as another. The same can be said about life's process in purpose. Everyone has a purpose, but the results and outcomes vary individually. That's why a single life is a time. There is only one of you throughout time and will not be again. There may be versions of you as offspring from the legacy you leave behind, but never again to be another YOU.

ENTERING A NEW TIME

There is so much in the details. Have you ever gone to an art exhibit and seen a Van Gogh up close? Have you ever studied a Monet up close? The fines strokes of the brush and how they lift off the canvas is stunning, but even in all their beauty, they do not begin to compare to the artistic creativity of our Father. God spared no details in his extravagance, and yet, we don't even notice the details. He wants us to find pleasure and delight in his creation. He wants us to reevaluate every three months; just take a moment to study yourself in the mirror. Father doesn't want us to stay there and concentrate on the wrinkles and sunspots. Oh no. He wants us to deal with what we find in the mirror that we see, the things that are in the soul of us.

He wants to purify us, and then allow us to enjoy the splendor of everything he provided through his covenant love. That's what he desires. It's not meant to be hard. There are hard times, sure, but if you're toiling earnestly, you're going to see some fruit. I don't do well with the toiling, but it's only for a season. Our time of toil is drawing to an end. Jesus will return to his people, his kingdom.

The time is here for something new, something different than what we've ever witnessed before. Will you recognize it when it is right in front of you or all around you? Be aware of changing times and seasons. Be willing to march to the beat of a different rhythm when it is time. Before my Father passed, I couldn't have known what was in store for my brother and me. Now, I can reflect back and see that even in my father's passing, God was raising something up from my brother and me with tremendous purpose. We could've made different choices. We could've gone back to life as it had been. God knew better. He made us better. Recognizing the changes of times and seasons is a crucial part of understanding your purpose in the world today and how you're called to effect it.

SEASONS

Seasons are the cycles within time that repeat. This will resemble a circle. This gives us the opportunity to reevaluate previous decisions, learn from our experiences and improve process throughout time. Why do so many say history repeats itself? There is typically so much time between some seasons that we do not learn from the previous generations. We do not give an account to pass on our successes and failures to our offspring, to honor the lessons that time has taught us. Therefore, we inevitably repeat failures. This is a reason for disciplining others, so they learn from the past and do not make the same mistakes. This is why we must write down our vision and purpose so that others will know and work with you to complete what has been started.

My father lived for a time of seventy-one years. His five-year disease of pulmonary fibrosis was for a season. My father left a legacy of inheritance and he passed on what is to be continued through my brother and me. We will pass on what he, his father, and fathers before him started. The time may have ended with him, but seasons of his work bear fruit in us and our offspring. Think about what is being passed on to you.

THE FOUR SEASONS

In every season- Spring, Summer, Fall and Winter there is purpose. Spring is the time that the trees begin to bud. It is a sign of new fresh life. Summer is time when the crops are growing and preparing for harvest. Fall is harvest-time. The air is cool again. An overall sense of rest and accomplishment for a year fulfilled is embraced. Winter is the time that the roots grow stronger. It is a deep introspective work. Winter prepares us for casting new vision while tending to dead things from the previous year. As the strategy for the next year comes into focus, planning 'springs' into the right course of action in the next season. Goals for implementation throughout the entire year is top of mind. Within each of these four seasons are contained four fractional seasons: watch, prepare, wait, and act.

Watch to see the signs of change. Watch to see what direction the wind is blowing to see how it will affect what needs to be done. This will help you prepare.

Preparation is when you gather the information you need to be effective for the next season. You seek God and his plan to execute it with efficient and effective intention. You will also assess things from the previous season that will not be required or prove useful in the next season. If I've been working in the garden, those garden tools don't necessarily help me do the dishes after dinner. You may need rest, or you may need to gather provisions to bring you through the next season. You may find that what was effective in the last season isn't what you need for the new one. Wait for the Lord's timing before moving into the new. If you start to early, it can cause discouragement in or abortion of the assignment. If you wait too long, opportunities may be missed that produce growth and development necessary to complete a season. These kind of delays can hinder proper maturity.

Act on what God has prepared for you. Prove yourself worthy of the purpose spoken in 2 Timothy 4:7 by fighting a good fight, finishing the race, and keeping the faith. Watch, prepare, and wait for the time to act. Then act. Take a glance at where you've been to ensure you end up where you're supposed to be. Celebrate your progress.

Knowing the times and seasons and operating accordingly in them is an imperative part of the believer's lifestyle. Ecclesiastes 3 says there is a time and season for everything. There's a time to be born and a time to die. A time to plant and a time to uproot. A time to kill and a time to heal. Remember, we are spiritual warriors; there are times where we're called to take down dark principalities. There's a time to tear down and build. It's not fun when you come to one of those tearing down seasons—at least not for me.

There is a time to mourn and a time to dance. A time to scatter stones and a time to gather them. A time to embrace and a time to refrain. There are times I don't want to hug you—and even times I shouldn't. There's a time to tear up and a time to mend, a time to be silent and a time to speak. There's even a time to love and a time to hate.

There's a time to work and a time to rest, but what does the worker gain from his toil? I have seen the burden God has laid on men, for his yoke is easy and his burden is light. He has made everything beautiful in its time. He has also set eternity in the hearts of men. Yet, they cannot fathom what God has done from beginning to end. I know that there is nothing better for men than to be happy and to do good while they live. Every man may eat and drink and find satisfaction in his toil. It is the gift of God to find happiness in our toil. I know that everything God does will endure forever, and because of this, nothing can be added or taken away from it. God does this so men will remember him, love him, and keep his commandments.

SEASONS WITHIN SEASONS

Let's break this down a little more. In each season you have three months. So we see the seasons, as one, two, three, four, but in reality, God's seasons actually have four seasons in every quarter. Think winter, spring, summer, fall multiplied by four, except it's not necessarily winter, spring, summer, fall with God, it's your season to war or plant, your season to watch and tend, or your season to reap. You go through all four in a given season and then it starts over again. This shifts our whole paradigm. We have only been observing a reaping of once a year; we've been cutting our resources short because we haven't recognized that there is a reaping in every quarter. That's God's plan for Kingdom expansion.

I went years and years around the same mountain not getting anywhere? That was largely due to what I confessed and how I started a season. If I were to review previous personal February journal entries, I would likely see repeating patterns. If I admit to myself that I will see that cycle return again, then by the confession of my faith, I will see the same cycle return. Therefore, to change a patterned cycle, I must confess the change.

Times & Seasons

When I realized what was really happening, I was like, *Wait a minute! No, I'm not doing this anymore. God, I don't know what I have to change, but I don't want to do this 'February cycle' again. I want a new February.*

As soon as I asked, he answered. God began a work in my heart that February, and he started showing me issues that needed to be dealt with in my life. This was before I understood the power of my confession. Here is what I learned through this example: when we set our mind to change, it changes. Change comes much faster and easier with the help of Holy Spirit. I didn't change God's mind; I changed the condition of my heart and mind. When my heart wanted a change, then I followed my heart. Out of my mouth came the confession of my heart and a change was the product of that confession. The cycle was broken. A new and better way was set into motion. When I set myself on a new course, repenting of how I undermined my own purpose, turning and doing something different, lining myself up with the Word, guess what? I never had another February like those February's. This lesson taught me how to navigate my confessions to produce life and not curses.

Just imagine how much more your life can produce when you realize cycles of your own. The seasons allow us an opportunity to assess areas of strengths and weaknesses so we may grow and produce good fruit in the likeness of God's nature. Scripture tells us that we may be renewed every day through the Spirit and the washing of the Word. When we assess accurately through the knowledge, revelation, and counsel of the Lord, we judge ourselves and repent so we will grow in greater measure to be able to enjoy the season the Lord has us in at that moment.

God doesn't need to change; he's got it all figured out. Although how many times do we honestly need to take note of where we are and where we need to change? Do you remember your first vehicle? I don't know about you, but it took me a season or two to realize that I needed to be cognizant of how much oil was in my car. I learned that I shouldn't wait until my gas light was on "E" to fill up. I needed to occasionally inspect my tires, walk around my vehicle or have somebody look under the hood. We don't think about those things when we're so busy moving. We get in the car to go from point A to point B often forgetting to inspect or care for it. The same happens in our hearts. Busyness is a distraction from handling important matters, *Is there something I need to change? Where do I need some maintenance? What was poking me three weeks ago that didn't poke me a year ago?* When we become aware of these things and turn them over to Jesus, they become areas of refinement where we grow and move forward in our purpose.

Your life is blessed through the covenant of Jesus. Recognize your seasons and begin moving into the fullness of whatever time and season God has you in. See blessings manifest. Watch exponential provision manifest as you mature in purpose.

SEASONS OF SONSHIP

Sonship is a season of relationship where the "son", albeit son or daughter, disciple humbles themselves to a submissive position to be "fathered", by either a fathering or mothering individual or couple in leadership, for the purpose of maturing through discipleship. This is challenging for some because they've either never really had a father or mother figure in their life, or if they did, maybe wasn't the best example. Sometimes, the son or daughter is unteachable. It is the role of the fathering leader to give counsel, instruction, and correction. Correction without direction is NOT fathering.

A son must be postured to walk in the position of sonship with a teachable spirit in humility and accountability. It is not easy to take correction, but the instruction is for the greater good. When a son is unteachable, the father allows the son to move on as a prodigal son. If a father tries to control the son, then a drama triangle will inevitably ensue but is best avoided. It is a willful relationship of both the father and the son. A good father will have healthy offspring. A prodigal may leave, but those who return will eventually reflect the teachings of their father.

Being unteachable is when instruction is given to facilitate the best outcome, but the individual continues to do the same thing either through willful disobedience or being ignorant of accountability. Willful disobedience is when an individual justifies their behavior as being acceptable, unwilling to see the detriment of their choices while offering excuses as to why the results will turn out differently next time. Being ignorant of accountability is when an individual does not take personal responsibility for their actions and likely has not allowed healthy leadership in their life. Therefore, they don't recognize the need for it. They 'lone wolf' it. Accountability in sonship provides an environment to make mistakes safely or avoid them altogether. Being alone to learn according to the hard knocks leads to dangerous coping mechanisms. People that have grown up quite independently of discipleship or community typically run away from the help they really need and tend to ignore hard issues that lead to lawlessness and a false sense of security.

To properly father is to give correct information with instruction on how to facilitate the best results in character behaviors and accountability. A seasonal father will train up a son in the way he should go. He is to demonstrate this counsel with the heart of a teacher in the spirit of love. A father should be firm, not harsh; direct, not curt. A fathering leader will provide a nonjudgmental place for a son to mature making opportunity for the Son's advancement. A fathering leader will recognize what is to be accomplished in the season and see the course ahead for the Son. A father realizes that the time with this son is for a season being willing to release in the appropriate time.

The season of sonship serves a purpose in seasons of our lives as a process of promotion. It takes patience and trust for both parties to be accountable in humility to serve one another. The promotion for the son is to become a father and disciple many sons. For the father, it is a demonstration of honor to his fathering leaders to continue the legacy that began through his contrite heart that produced promotion. There may be many fathers in your life over time. You may have many sons throughout your life. All of them represent a season of purposeful intentionality within your lifetime.

Ancestral Purpose

DISCERNING TIMES AND SEASONS

Learning to discern spiritual changes in times and seasons is a gift from God. He gives this revelation and understanding to those who obey his commandments, showing themselves approved by the hearing and doing of what Scripture says just like it is stated in 2 Timothy 2:15. God has hidden this knowledge from the kingdom of darkness, so God's purpose is fulfilled. The tribe of Issachar was the one given the gift to be able to discern this knowledge. They knew when to plan, prepare, sow, reap, war, and rest. This discernment to recognize the changes of the times and seasons moves us into a realm of prosperity beyond provision. God proves his covenant with his children through the times and seasons.

Crispin and I moved to the coast July 2015. We knew God sent us to begin a ministry, but we didn't know what it was going to look like. Our assignment came after a season of intense warfare as we sowed everything and then some. On May 8, 2013, we buried my father. Four years later on the same day, our ministry on the coast was federally recognized. There is significance to this. The Lord was showing us that while one significant thing was buried, another was birthed. When my father passed on, so did his mantle. A season within a specific time completely fulfilled an aspect of our purpose. I have no better illustration of this than my testimony with my father and brother and how it all fits into God's purposes and plans for us and his kingdom.

My brother had been stationed in Djibouti in 2004 with the Army Special Forces. For those of you who don't know, Djibouti is not a nice area, and the gradual effects of the climate and warfare started to change my brother. While in Djibouti, my only sibling renounced his fellowship with the Lord. When he came home, we discovered he suffered from PTSD. My wonderful brother had turned into quite a different person when he was triggered into episodes of violent behavior. Due to these unexpected harmful outbursts, I felt as though I could not have a personal relationship with him anymore. I still loved him, but the relationship proved dangerous. I prayed for his deliverance and salvation with the hope that we would be a family restored.

When my brother was on deployment, he could receive calls occasionally. On one of these calls, I prophesied to him. I remember that prophecy as clearly as if it were yesterday. I remember seeing him in the spirit stepping off a private jet, wearing a robe that reminded me of the Biblical account of Joseph, but it was more in the form of a modern hand-tailored silk suit. It wasn't really rainbow colored, but I knew what it signified in the vision. I told him he was going to travel the world sharing the gospel and that his colored suit represented his redemptive gifts. I saw him traveling the world and people were being healed and born again. He was emptying hospitals with his healing anointing. He verbally rejected the prophecy and told his wife and I that he wasn't sure he even believed in God anymore, but I knew what I had seen. I was sure of what was to be.

Fast forward to May 2012, my father was diagnosed with pulmonary fibrosis. In June, I found myself in the doctor's office with him to receive a treatment plan. It was my daughter's birthday, and I just wanted some good news. Instead, as the doctor scrolled through my father's medical notes, I saw where his primary doctor had made an original diagnosis—several years earlier. Pulmonary Fibrosis is typically a five-year disease, and he was coming into his final year. His primary physician never told him.

In disbelief of what my eyes were seeing, I pointed at the screen and asked the pulmonary physician what that comment meant. He saw it, fell back in his chair, and we both went pale. The doctor tossed his glasses on the desk. He would have to rethink the treatment plan. My dad sat on the other side of the room with my mom, seeing our reactions, looked at us and said, *What's going on?* As the pulmonary specialist regained his composure, he gently explained to my father and mother.

The diagnosis really changed my dad's perspective on life and his faith. He started asking questions one might ask when facing death, *Am I really saved?* being one of them. You can live a life fully devoted to the Lord, but there may be moments when no matter the relationship, you still have questions. When Jesus was in the Garden of Gethsemane, perhaps he was thinking, *Is this real? Can I pinch myself and this not be true?*

Just as Jesus's death and resurrection produced new life for all who would come to know him, the Lord actually used this time to do a transformative work in my brother's life. As soon as he heard the news, things started to shift in his life slowly but surely. My entire family was in a season of warfare and transformation.

During this same year, I had a son who was fighting a brutal custody battle. Crispin and I would travel long hours through the night to help as his visitations were several states away. We would literally drive six hours each way one weekend, return home for a week, drive eight hours for another weekend to assist my mom with dad's home care, repeat visitation weekend and spent the last weekend of each month at home with my high school senior. Wash, rinse, repeat for a year. Crispin sometimes had to travel in other directions from this routine for his job.

My brother was having his experience, and I was having mine. When death happens close to you, it seems as though time stands still for a moment. It's like you are in a bubble where nothing else in the world is happening. Yet to everyone else, it's life as usual.

Dad's passing was peaceful. It allowed our family to cocoon together in a way that only Father- God could orchestrate.

The following day after my father's passing, my brother asked if he could wash my feet. I consented. As he began, he said that Jesus made him a changed man and he asked me to forgive him. Having forgiven him years earlier, I acknowledged his release.

Within a few hours, I had lost a father and regained a brother. My father wanted his children reconciled. My brother and I hadn't had a relationship in almost ten years, and now everything was capable of being restored. It was beautiful. From there, my brother went back to school for his doctorate, and began to travel the world preaching the gospel, healing people, and prophesying wherever opportunity allowed.

When my father passed, his mantle shifted onto my brother and me. Perhaps it was my father's unfulfilled destiny passed on as well as a mantle.

Meanwhile God was getting ready to place me in a position of authority but first there were some things needing restoration and being placed in order. From May to August, I would mourn the loss of dad, help my mother transition in a new life without my father, be present for the graduation and start of college of our youngest child. We even witnessed the victory of my son's custody battle. As I participated in the transition of the times and seasons, the Lord included a season of rest and closure for me before he brought me onboard with his next assignment –that which brought us to the coast.

God was doing something new, but I had to be willing to move into the change. I had to be willing to move into the new season which would usher in a new time. I had an inheritance to claim. I'm not necessarily talking about money. There was a new piece of Kingdom purpose reserved with my name on it, passed down through the generations of my father.

Taking up our father's mantle catapulted my brother and me into the 'new'. The 8th of May marks that significant point in time where God shifted things into an acceleration of his plans and purposes for my father, my brother, and me. God is showing honor to my father for raising us up in the way we should go through his children. It is the legacy of the wheel within the wheel: Father to father, Son to son. My brother and I embraced the mantle of my father in honor of him. The covenant is demonstrated through the blessings that manifest around us.

My story is only one aspect of the fulfilling of legacy. My father's name was well established and widely recognized in business and government across several regions. As such, there were entrepreneurial and governmental assignments passed on to his children and grandchildren. The mantle of my father's legacy offered dominion in several areas of influence in several territories. The same is true of the kingdom's covenantal principles of the seed, land, and livelihood through the Sower and the Reaper on a generational line. Each life is a season in time following the pattern of the wheel within a wheel: All are of the same origin, yet as one aspect dies another carries on anew.

Every bit of what was before, what is now, and what will be is part of my original intent. How I steward it determines the magnitude of portion fulfilled. It is my purpose. It all works to fulfill my destiny. This was a piece of my purpose that hadn't come to fulfillment or maturity until the passing of my father. The intentionality of purpose changed yet stayed the same. It is in the nature of God. I don't know what's next, and I don't need to know. If I need to be tilling the ground, then my mind needs to be on tilling the ground, making sure my rows are straight. That's what this season is about. My time has a beginning and an end. Yet through my children, it continues. I have one time, but many seasons. I have one destiny, but many different smaller pieces of intentionality that give purpose to my life within God's purpose. You do too.

When you're in a shift of intentionality, and you're seeing things change in ways that you cannot explain, it's because you're stepping into a new season that God intentioned from before the foundation of the world.

ROMANS 8:27-28
God the searcher of our heart, knows fully our longings, yet he also understands the desires of the Spirit, because the Holy Spirit passionately pleads before God for us, his holy ones, in perfect harmony with God's plan and our destiny. So we are convinced that every detail of our lives is continually woven together to fit into God's perfect plan of bringing good into our lives, for we are his lovers who have been called to fulfill his designed purpose.

Whether you find that you are in a new era of time, in a new season, or both, prayer is the key that unlocks the door of promotion in Jesus and humility is its threshold.

We have the ability to unlock the purpose God gave us through our intentioned humble service as a son of God in our appointed time.

Isaiah 22:22 says, *I will place on his shoulder the key to the house of David; what he opens no one can shut, and what he shuts no one can open.*

When reading this verse, I see the bolt lock of a door. It is a lock that requires two simultaneous keys to turn and unlock it; the keys represent scripturally based prayers also called weapons of warfare. One of those keys is Jesus who is constantly interceding for us. The second key is us. Once the door is unlocked, nothing is withheld. God wants us to desire what he desires, that's what relationship with him looks like. His love is perfect, and we have access to all of it through prayer and our relationship with him.

Jesus told us to love one another greater than the love we have for ourselves. When we demonstrate this love through working together for his purposes, we unlock more gifts of God and build up the kingdom of God. Let's say you and I both have salt in our hands. Once we put our salt together and then divide it up again, there is no way to tell one from the other. The salt would be completely blended. I have some of your salt and you have some of mine. Similarly, we strengthen each other when we allow our gifts and callings to work together. That's covenant. That's relationship. Salt is covenant, and when we align ourselves together, we are in covenant with one another. It's not a dirty word, it's a heavenly union.

Purpose is fulfilled in the times and seasons through relationships. Who are the people who have had the greatest impact in your life? Did it lead you to areas of accomplishment or promotion? Did some relationships prevent you from accelerating in your purpose?

Are you beginning to see how it all fits together yet? Well, hold on, because there is more. Perhaps you have already started moving in one or more of these aspects of God's times and seasons to propel

Ancestral Purpose

your purpose. If so, then you can already measure the difference the slightest implementation can bring. This is exciting!

It is important to remember, you matter. Your purpose matters. Throughout the ages of time there is and will be only one YOU. What is the legacy you want to leave behind? Will your life reflect your purpose? Will you impact others through your relationships over the times and seasons in your own life? You hold the key to your own destiny. Make your time and seasons accountable to your purpose.

KINGDOM

PURPOSE

7

INFLUENTIAL PURPOSE

Over the next three chapters, I'll try to convey the original intent of God's purpose for us in the earth through the covenant of Kingdom Principle through the seed – as your birthright. As a Sower, the land will produce provision of covenant. As a Reaper, abundant blessings will result through obedience. My heart is to show you how God's kingdom operates and how you may apply this to your own life. It is very important to use the Study Guide during this section to really see how it all fits together. As you read each chapter in this section, consider the following: The ecclesia of God as two parts in one as the seed; 1) Use the times and seasons to direct us when and how to do what is to be done and then; 2) Reap harvests of seed, land and livelihood through kingdom influence as part of your birthright and blessing.

REALMS OF INFLUENCE

The Seven Mountains of Influence concept is built around a thought that there are seven primary realms of influence within society: religion, government, family, arts and entertainment, media, economy, and education. It is by understanding the spiritual side of these physical entities that we hope to reclaim them for their intended purpose: to advance the kingdom of God. I used to think there were three realms of influence through government, family, and education, but 'tis no longer the case. However, there is merely one sphere of influence in God's kingdom. God is not religious. He is God, Supreme Ruler, Creator, Teacher, Father of all creation, Provider, All in all. When we consider God's original intention for his kingdom, the realm of influence is sought and found in him through covenant. Therefore, his realm of influence is in relational government as a kingdom with his family of heirs.

When God made man, it was about the relationship. It was his primary intention. He gave us life, the land to take dominion over, blessed our seed and commanded us to be fruitful and multiply his image on the earth. God established his government in this world through his family—the most influential mountain. The family had the authority that was given by God. Adam, being the first created son of God, was the first to receive dominion. Today, through Jesus, we are family. This allows us citizenship in the mountain of Zion.

Now we know what the seven mountains of influence are and can see them in the world around us, but when we look at Revelation, it shows us their fate. We know that Revelation is the end of the beginning and the beginning of the end; it's our guide to keep us on track. Knowing the ending of the story is like painting by numbers. You see the picture from the start, but when it's filled in, it reveals the picture in a beautiful new way. When we keep filling in certain places in our lives with the colors of our redemptive gifts, then it becomes a beautiful picture of completion, just like the book of Revelation.

While Revelation is our guide to the future, the New Testament is saying, *Jesus has come back! He gave us the keys to the Kingdom and now we are supposed to restore it on earth as it is in Heaven.* Jesus Himself prayed those words to the Father. Everything that we do is to glorify and edify God and his Kingdom both on earth and in heaven. There is nothing that is not meant to give glory to God.

When we go to Revelation 17 to read about the harlot and the beast, the harlot is described as being covered in the blood of the saints. This metaphoric shedding of blood has occurred through thousands of years. This passage serves to show us that there are broken blood covenants throughout time. A harlot does not represent the relationship in covenant, as a man and his wife, but rather these two things: *breaching covenant* while appealing to one's senses via an *unlawful economic transactions*. Repeatedly in scripture, we see how the unrighteous kingdom seduces believers away from covenant with God. 1) A transaction is made at an individual's point of agreement with unrighteousness. A) An individual will do something that violates their covenant with God. B) The indulgence brings them a moment of temporary satisfaction, but there is some kind of exchange made involving blood, food, or money. We can rename 'indulgence' as compromise, lawlessness, or transgression. 2) It costs them the inheritance of covenantal blessing until repentance is made and covenant with God is restored.

Examples: Sampson and Delila, Esau and Jacob, Eli and his sons, Saul and the seer, David and Bathsheba, Ananias and Sapphira, Judas Iscariot. You can likely find more throughout the history of your nation and generational line.

UNRIGHTEOUS RULERS

Through the Babylonian, Egyptian and Greek influences perverting bloodlines throughout their dominions, the dark kingdom gained much influence within the world. One such ruler was Nimrod.

Nimrod, the king of Babylon desired to seek knowledge from the fallen. Nimrod worshipped these as deities, and desired to be like them. How do we know this? Go back to Genesis. After one third of the stars fell, it says the sons of God fell in love with the daughters of man. They created this sort of mutant in the land called Nephilim. The fallen and their mutants are from where Greek mythology and all other deities originate. This co-mingling of blood perverted man's seed. That's why God spoke to them and said, *Don't marry these.* The blood had been made impure. God would bring His Son through a pure unmutated, undefiled seed.

The Antichrist kingdom culture is slowly turning up the heat of the water hoping you'll enjoy its warm relaxing temperature until you are completely cooked. It's time to jump out of that pot and help yourself to the truth. Currently, the United Nations desires one mountain for world domination. For now, they are using the seven spheres of influence to accomplish their goal. There is a synergistic movement that uses the media mountain to invoke fear and confusion. Then they condemn truth using politics, art, and entertainment. The economy is being manipulated to produce fear and a dependency on government instead of free enterprise. Mainstreaming means bullying people to accept unrighteousness rather than to love what is holy. The Antichrist spirit only allows education to be taught to promote what they want taught. They change the facts of history to accommodate their own narrative. The Antichrist may win for a while but will not win the war. You can read Revelation and see for yourself. God's Kingdom will rule and reign forever.

ABRAHAM'S SEED

When Abraham went against the covenant that God had spoken over him and tried to do things himself, I believe his heart was right, he just didn't think God was up to the challenge. Quite honestly, I'm not sure Abraham and Sarah felt like they were up to it either.ABraham beds his wife's maid servant and out of that comes Ishmael. God blessed Ishmael because he was Abraham's son, but his bloodline was not pure enough to birth the seed of God. When Ishmael came of age, he was sent off to the land of his mother's heritage—a land of idolatry. Ishmael represents the perverted bloodline.

The message of God's love for his people was repeated through Abraham and his bloodline. Ishmael heard it and knew it. He was raised in that household for a season. Ishmael was circumcised and followed after God. He knew what God had spoken, but somewhere in his generational line things changed, and out of that came a new seed of religion. It is growing and perpetuating in the earth through Ishmael's seed.

Like Ishmael, many who know the love of God have had their spiritual seed blended with some form of idolatry. Be hopeful. There is a remnant with the pure unadulterated blood of Jesus through their repentance. The remnant is growing, and they will be spotless. God is going to use those pure spiritual seeds called the

Kingdom Purpose

Bride of Christ to overturn the false structures that have sewn perverted influences in the nations. He will bring Mount Zion to earth for a pure and holy mountain.

KINGDOM CULTURE

Can we agree that we have been in a society under global influences for hundreds of years as a nation? Have we not been influenced by language, fashion, art, politics, education, religion, and family influences? I believe we discussed these types of influences in the first chapter of Identity. Yes, there are influences in our life that shape our decisions, behaviors, and lifestyle. God desires to live with us, through us, and have his being in us. God desires to be our only sphere of influence.

The teaching of the Seven Mountain Influence tells us that we are to go into these realms with the nature of Christ. Using our gifts and talents, we are to make an impact in these areas. We are to operate in different aspects of each mountain; overtly, covertly, serving, and ruling. To be effective in overturning these mountains from the enemy, we need to be able to hear the Lord, know our identity, identify our purpose according to our gifts, talents, and passions, and move through the times and seasons with understanding. This creates a lifestyle of intentionality as you trust and obey the Lord in all his ways. When you do what you are created to do, it is amazing how simple life can be. The perks are that miracles, signs and wonders will follow you. It just can't get any better.

The seven run together and play into each other more than we think. Israel was only given God's government rule when he gave the two tablets of the law. He offered relationship when he invited them to join him around the mountain, but they refused him. Instead, they went off and built a golden calf.

When God was there with Moses, the mountain represented the kingdom of God. It wasn't about religion or politics. God was saying to his people, *I want you to really understand my heart. Yes, this is the law but if you understand my heart, you will understand my government. These are precepts that are real, but my heart is that you would love and honor me. Then I will pour out my blessings on you.* Relationships are big with God. But it doesn't stop there though. We also need to love one another. We're all God's children. He doesn't love any of us more than another. His love is reflected through his blessing as we obey, so we are blessed. It's not contingent on how well we live our lives, but if we cut off the blessing of God, life's going to look pretty grim.

Now that we can identify these seven mountains in our society, and we see the enemy running amuck on all of them, what do we do? Should we do anything? Well, friend, I think it's more apparent now than ever that we need to go in with the authority of Jesus and reclaim these mountains for his name's sake.

RETAKE THE MOUNTAINS

My son said something to me several years ago that really caught my attention. *Mom,* he said. *People don't understand where our media and entertainment are headed. If we don't start taking the media mountain and the mountain of arts and entertainment, we're going to come to a point where those areas of influence are completely controlled by the enemy.* We can already see this happening. The television industry takes you through this process of giving their perspective to change your mind and make you think a certain way. Isn't that how marketing works? *Come here, buy our stuff, it's better, it's less expensive.* Our nation is coming to the point where it is controlled by whoever controls the message on the screen.

When my son told me that, I grieved and began to see the image of Christ standing condemned before all the people of a nation screaming, *Crucify him!* What had Jesus done? He was an innocent man, but what about the man they wanted to free in his stead? He was a convicted murderer, and yet, they let him go. They killed the Messiah and freed the murderer. Doesn't this start to sound familiar?

Where are we headed? What does our future look like if we do not go into the mountains and claim them for the Kingdom? What happens if we do not turn the tides? Where do we begin? What do we do? What is our part? We have taken political correctness to such an extreme that truth is discouraged in our country.

I have a gentleman friend who's been in ministry since 1999, a man with a real fathering spirit. He was the one who actually taught me about inner healing and deliverance. He will see a wounded person—male or female—and he will give that fathering to them that they never had. He can't be that for everybody, but he knows how to approach hurting people with a true father's heart. But I'm sad to say that his ministry is not as effective as it used to be, because even a side hug or private conversation with someone could label him a pervert or someone who makes people uncomfortable. Fathers can't be fathers anymore because of potentially offending somebody, when all they really want to do is show them the Father's heart.

What have we come to? I'm not discounting these men and women's hurts, but this is how we got here. Follow the trail and eventually you'll find the reason. So I just keep asking, *Alright, Papa, where do I go from here?*

We have to win the mountains back. What started out as the Babylonian mountains are now supposed to be ours. We can go overtly or covertly, but it's important that we begin on our knees and gain our strategies from God and let him lead us into battle.

Ron has the heart of a father with an evangelistic ministry, but his ministry is not going to look like what it did ten years ago. The word of God does not change, but the situations around us do. The way Ron approaches ministry must change with the times and seasons we're in and it has to be different, it has to go beyond expectation. We have to be in front of the curve to know what to do and know how it's going to be received before we approach. Our strategies must be sound.

We're turning these mountains. If we're going to have one mountain again—Mount Zion—it will be in the order of Melchizedek, just like Jesus. God was never religious; not in one iota of his being. I once took a class on the names of God, and in it, the instructor said that to even call God "God" is an insult because he was not a created being. The "little g's" were all created, but God is the Creator. He didn't establish religion, he established his government, and he did it through the relationship of his family. That is where we're headed. That is what living a life eternal with Jesus looks like. Jesus is going to sit on the mountain of New Jerusalem, and he will rule from there and we are going to have our dominion and fellowship with him as family and joint heirs. That's what the Word says.

INFLUENCE MOUNTAINS

There just is not enough study done on the topic of the Seven Mountains of Influence. After digging for weeks, I finally came to the point where I was like, *Holy Spirit, what do you want to say to me about this?* If only I'd started there. What the Holy Spirit gave me aligned perfectly with the truth I know in my heart. Holy Spirit revelation doesn't always look like what we think it will. Even in the redemptive gifts when we're looking at, say, the giver, that their realm of influence will likely be in the business or economic mountain, but it makes sense because givers establish a platform for businesses because they utilize every resource as an aspect of commerce. When you give and you release, you release the blessings of God, which means you have more to give. It's a precept of God.

When we understand the precepts of God, we begin to flow in those blessings and that's what we're trying to demonstrate in the mountains. By being who God says we are and doing what God tells us to do, God's glory will be released. Changes will occur. He'll do this through short-term and long-term assignments. Sometimes we have special assignments. Crispin and my dad both used to work for the government. We had a lot of involvement and influence on that mountain. I don't necessarily claim the government mountain, but we've left our mark.

Several years ago, Crispin, my husband, served on a national council in DC, but his assignment is short and precise; it's one mission and one goal on one mountain. On the governmental mountain there are people going up through the center, working their way to the top. They're like plant pollen; they're kind of like the servants in the mountains. They're role is to move in and out without hardly being noticed. They're praying over desks or making small changes for our benefit, and we don't even know they're there. We may not find out about it for years, but it's the little nudges that help put us back in the right direction.

You have several little targets but it's all one purpose. The message behind what you do doesn't change, but it may take that message into a classroom, a hospital, nursing home, business or into a mall. One's purpose stays consistent, but the mountain one's feet are on may change. Remember, focuses can and do change periodically with times and seasons.

My heart is to see people walk in their purpose and fulfill the destiny that was birthed in them before the foundation of the world. Before you were even known in your mother's womb, God knew you, and that purpose was there. If you're struggling to know what that is, all you need to do is go back to that time and say, *God, what did you birth in me that I'm supposed to be fulfilling now?*

Has anyone completed their purpose to the fullest that Christ did? It appears as though the bulk of his ministry was in that last three years, but it really wasn't. He had to grow up. There were things that Jesus had to learn. It didn't change his purpose, but he was on different mountains at different times. He was on a family mountain being educated. He was on the business mountain because he was a carpenter like his father. He moved from mountain to mountain during those years, but yet only his ministry is noted.

Jesus' message was not lost. His death and resurrection was part of his purpose all along. Yet, he journeyed through life and maturation just as we all do. When those last three years came and John the Baptist took him under the water and pulled him back up, all of those giftings just started flowing. Then when he left and was tempted, he was able to stand. He had to learn how to be tempted because this was the time, he was going to give an account and it had to matter. Everything mattered at that point. Everything was on the line.

Believe it or not, where you are right now matters. This is your place of decision. You think salvation was a place of decision? Oh, man, that's where the decisions really begin. We have to decide how we plan to live the rest of our lives for the Lord.

BRACE FOR IMPACT

I was talking to an intercessor friend of mine the other day, and I was sharing with her that I had the opportunity to pray at the National Day of Prayer. She asked me how it went, and I replied, *Well, I had an inner struggle. I was debating whether I should say something easy on the ears so that I'll be invited back or if I should say what I feel led to say.* In the end, I went with the latter; I never knew if I'd have the platform to pray again. There was no compromise. Even if it meant that doors would close on my face, I had to take that risk because my doors aren't opened by me anyway. I just did what I was told to do. I'm challenging you to test your limits.

SEVEN MOUNTAINS IN THE WORD

I'm going to go over the seven mountains that we find in scripture. I really struggled with how they related to the redemptive gifts within their Biblical significance, but I prayed over the meaning of their names, locations, and how they aligned with the redemptive gifts. This is where I landed through the direction of Holy Spirit. The redemptive gifts have to do with the way that God established them, not how we establish them. God's ways are not our ways.

MT. ARARAT

We can start with Mount Ararat, *meaning the curse reversed.* Covenant was restored with a rainbow. In Genesis 8 this is where Noah's Ark landed—or is believed to have landed. He landed there in the seventh month on the seventeenth day.

The thing about Ararat is that it's part of a chain of mountains. When you think about the chain, you think about the seed, right? Because you plant a row and one springs forth, then another; this is what I felt the Lord was saying. This is the family mountain. God started with his family in a garden. He started with his creation; that's the foundation. Creation was preserved. Noah's family represent the first seeds after the flood, and through that, God made a covenant with man: his rainbow, the seven colors of the redemptive gifts reflecting God's covenant of provision.

The servant redemptive brings healing to the land and servants know how to honor the land and livestock. When he brought Noah to Ararat, he had an animal of every kind—the seed of every kind. I don't think it actually says that, but he didn't come empty handed because he had grain for all the animals—he was in the ark for a long time. When that rainbow fell over that beautiful mountain where they were nestled, and they began to take their dominion, rule and procreate the way that they were ordered to in the beginning, the blessing of the servant was fulfilled. Their boundaries were secured, and they were given much freedom to expand.

MT. MORIAH

Mount Moriah, *means chosen by Jehovah*, is found in Genesis 22. This is where Isaac was spared from being sacrificed. Abraham had longed for this son and finally he came, but then God spoke to him and said, *Abraham, take him up the mountain, it's time for the sacrifice.* Abraham must have been frantic. *What am I going to do? I love this boy. How am I going to get the stars out of a dead child?*

When the time came, Abraham was obedient to God. He took Isaac up the mountain, laid him down on the altar and prepared to strike. But suddenly the angel of the Lord appeared and said, *Wait, you don't have to do this. A sacrifice has been provided.* Sure enough, that mountain yielded a sacrifice for Abraham so that Isaac did not have to be the resource. Because of that, Mount Moriah is the economic mountain for the giver redemptive gift. The blessing of this mountain is freedom to accumulate resources year to year, generation to generation. This would fall into order with Abraham's prophecy. Isaac was supposed to be the seed, but a ram was found in the land that could take his place. God provided it there; he gave Abraham the resources.

MT. SINAI / HOREB

Mount Sinai, also referred to as Mount Horeb—can be read about in the book of Exodus. This is referred to as the *Mountain of God*. The names' root meanings are *thorny, desolate, or to lay waste*. Moses goes up there and is given the two tablets of the law, the ten commandments.

This is the ruler or administrative redemptive gift on the education mountain. The blessing of this mountain is the ability to establish synergistic social structures that establish free-living cultures. Those tablets were supposed to tell them about the precepts of God and teach them about his heart. It wasn't about the law as much as it gave his people boundaries for safety, security, and covenant. God's heart is to love. It's all about the relationship between us and him, and then our relationship with others. But they didn't learn from that; they kept making mistake after mistake and God had to purify them with blood over and over again. It became a vicious cycle of sin and atonement, but never reconciliation.

MT. PISGAH / NEBO

Mount Pisgah, *meaning cleft*, also known as Nebo, *meaning prophet*, is the place where God took Moses to see the promised land. This is the government mountain because Moses is establishing the future for Israel. The redemptive gift for this mountain is in the meaning of its name. Its blessing is security from intrusion. God left enemies to be conquered so the Israelites would love the land and have a sense of ownership. Moses was called to be the deliverer and spokesperson for the Israelites. They finally reached their place of purpose and were transitioning from the wilderness into the promised land; a land they were meant to rule. So from there, Moses sent out the ten witnesses to bring back the report of the Lord. But eight didn't report what Moses saw. They did not prophesy their future and come into agreement with the

Kingdom Purpose

Word of the Lord. There is something to be said here for stepping into your purpose in the appropriate time and season.

MT. CARMEL

Next, is Mount Carmel, *the garden-land*. When I stepped onto this mountain for the first time, I could immediately feel spiritual contention over it. The blessing for this media mountain operating in the exhorter redemptive is the ability to systematically develop areas of greatest potential. Queen Jezabel was exploiting leaders and peoples of Israel, forcing folks to idolatry, and demanded all the attention.

In 1 Kings 18, we read this is where Elijah calls down the fire on the altar. He threw down the gauntlet to the priests of Baal. Elijah was a prophet who used his place of authority to establish God's Kingdom order for Israel. Elijah realized that the people of God were not thriving and most of the prophets of God had been executed. He had had enough. Elijah called the meeting to order, and God showed up! Hundreds of false prophets died by the sword and a short time later, and Jezebel became dogfood.

MT. HERMON & MT. TABOR

These are two separate mountains. Mount Hermon is a large mountainous territory which means *a sanctuary, sacred or a breastplate; to consecrate through destruction, grey headed, and eyes of the nation*. Whereas Mount Tabor is a ridge along Nazareth. Its root meaning *is to be broken into pieces, crushed violently (fig), or to break forth or rupture like a fig; fragile*. It is argument that one of these two mountains was the Mountain of Transfiguration. Peter, James and John were there with Jesus, and this is where they at first only saw him as a man. Then Abba Father came as a cloud covering them and instantly Jesus was transfigured standing with Moses and Elijah. The disciples are in awe; they didn't know what to think. In their meanings, it is conveyed in my spirit that these two mountains convey symbolically the Tree of the Knowledge of Good and Evil. God alone is Judge. Holy Spirit becomes the Judge within us to help us know in purity what is right or wrong. This is our spiritual/religious mountain operating through the teacher redemptive. The blessing of these special places is the ability to enthrone Jesus on the land.

MT. OLIVE

The last mountain of the seven is Mount Olive—or Olivette—found in the books of Matthew, Mark, Luke and John. Olive trees represent the Tree of Life that was in the Garden of Eden. It also represents the oil of God's anointing. The oil represents the fire of God expressed through the infilling of Holy Spirit.

This mountain is where Jesus went to pray before he was betrayed in the Garden of Gethsemane—a small mountain in a beautiful garden of olive trees. Then Jesus walked through the Via Dolorosa and that's all along there between the low place and the high place. He ended up on the side of the mountain right outside Jerusalem. It's still a mountain, but it's on the side of Jerusalem and this is where Jesus was when he cried out to his Father. This is the mountain of possessing the birthright.

As Jesus went through his last days, knowing he'd be betrayed, he took communion. Later, he went into the Garden of Gethsemane, where he cried out saying, *Just let this cup pass from me. This doesn't taste good. This doesn't feel good, and I don't like it.* I know those feelings and you do too. We've all been there. *Does this really have to be me? Do I really have to go through this? Isn't there another way to teach me?* Jesus was in the olive press. Nevertheless, Jesus yielded himself completely to his father and he did not defend himself. *If this is the way I have to do it, then so be it. I will defend your honor. I will represent the love that has come to set men free.*

We can truly see we see the love of Jesus through the events that transpired there. Truly this is the mercy redemptive gift being demonstrated, not because of any weakness, but because of his strength. As Holy Spirit came at Pentecost, it was on this very mountain. For this, we see an expression of heart like none other. A story of the ages is expressed through the fulfillment of what took place there on this arts and entertainment mountain.

Kingdom Purpose

How do we express what's in our heart? Through poetry, song, dance and arts. Jesus was expressing. It didn't look like celebration at the time, but our victory was won when he died on that cross and rose again, and that was all on that mountain. We can now rejoice with eternal song that will resound through the ages that he has risen again. He took the keys of hell, broke the gates and conquered death. And for that, we can sing and dance and cry out to him for the rest of eternity.

ACTIVATED INFLUENCE

In this chapter, we've talked about the spheres of influence in our culture today and how they developed within our society through the fallen nature of man. We compared those structures from centuries ago and now. Then we paralleled these mountains with the redemptive gifts with actual historical places realizing that the land also has redemptive gifts. Perhaps now you too can identify the blessings in spheres of influence to know how to mobilize, pray, and bring them into righteous function as we utilize our redemptive authority as the ecclesia.

The ecclesia is responsible for restoring the original intent upon the land by identifying the sin on the land. We apply the blood of Jesus to the land to bring the land and its territory back on the redemptive intention by repenting and forgiving the trespasses of man and his sin. Once the land has been cleansed, we bless the land to operate as God designed it. This overturns any curse that has bound the land from its covenant of provision. Take a look around to see what is on the land where you live. Identify what is right or wrong. If it can be acknowledged, then we believe as we are entrusted with the truths regarding heavenly things. We are to pray into these things we see to bring the reformation needed to restore God's Kingdom on earth. We are His servants to do His heart's work. Repentance and forgiveness are the governmental tools we use to restore the pure original intention into the land as we apply the blood of Jesus. Then once the land has been cleansed through prayer, we release the land into God's purpose.

Influential Purpose

Redemptive purpose on the land is connected to the seven Redemptive Gifts: Perceiver (Prophet), Servant, Teacher, Exhorter, Giver, Administrative (Ruler), and Compassion (Mercy). The way these gifts appear on the land will directly affect the way that the Seven Areas of Influence or Mountains operate. The land will either operate on the right side of its gifting or on the wrong side. Presently, we are going to talk about how they land is affected when operating righteously. The study of the Redemptive Gifts on the land is more commonly known as Redemptive Cities, but it is understood that a Redemptive City could mean Cities, Counties, Regions, States, and Nations. I'm going to go into some brief descriptions to help you understand how to identify the redemptive gift on your land and what could be its stronghold. People open the doors to the iniquities. First, take a look at examples of people operating improperly in their redemptive gift before we apply how it looks on the land:

> **Prophet/Perceiver**: right of individuals. A focus on rights of individuals to the exclusion of responsibility. Example- Abortion attributes rights of mother verses responsibility to the baby.
>
> **Servant:** peace at any cost. Submits to victimization because it is less painful than fighting while passively empowering predators and damaging society. Example: School not addressing reports of bullying, so bullied student brings gun to school and shoots innocents.
>
> **Teacher:** selective responsibility. Falling into a religious activity verses calling. Example: A son of a preacher was called to be an attorney at nineteen, but pastors father's church instead.
>
> **Exhorter:** denial on two levels; confronting sin and embrace discomfort. A music minister becomes a predator towards a musician, but pastor won't address for fear of losing the music minister.

Kingdom Purpose

Giver: control. A giver uses funds appropriated for another department rather than following the protocol for acquiring the funds.

Ruler: exploitation. The children of the city came together to raise funds for a new playground, but the city sold the proposed land to a developer.

Mercy: stubbornness with a focus toward self-gratification rather than obedience. The Civil Engineers reported that corrections should be made on a strip on land for city safety, but the city decided they would not be able to comply because the repairs would interfere with the season's tourism.

Understanding how to identify a healthy redemptive gift versus an unhealthy redemptive gift will help you determine how to correct it in yourself, others, and the land. When the iniquity of mankind has been transferred to the land through man's unrighteous covenants, there will be cause and effect. Soon, man is either tempted in this same iniquity or becomes part of it because so much of it is on the land. Once the ecclesia has been effective in breaking off the strongholds on the land, the land gets better and begins to look more like its original intent and the people of that land will gradually become free from the iniquity as well.

In the next chapter, we go into great detail about this subject. Please make sure you have your Study Guide handy as these concepts are not widely discussed or taught. You may need to make plenty of notes. There may be some aspects to this training that will simply have to be 'caught' as you begin to identify these things in your own territories.

8

R̲e̲d̲e̲m̲p̲t̲i̲v̲e̲ ̲P̲u̲r̲p̲o̲s̲e̲

The reason God placed you where you are, is because you have been given the authority in this land in this time to accomplish His purposes. The spiritual realm is not affected by historic or political boundaries, but how we wield our authority in Christ for a specific purpose in during a specific time.

The way to determine the Redemptive Design on your land is through research. A continent's identity is the foundation of the land, then the national identities, next that land's regional identity, and so on. For instance, your nation may be Redemptive City (Design) of Perceiver, while the state or region could be an Administrative (Ruler) Design, but your city may be a Giver City. How does all of this work together? That continent will demonstrate things from border to border than connect all across that continent. Next, each nation will demonstrate a new series of traits. Then the process continues down to cities. Neighboring cities impact a city's Redemptive Design. You ready? Okay.

Start from the ground up by beginning with the city where you live. Check out your city's website. Take inventory of its appearance, its highlights, and areas of focus. Do they use this site to acknowledge particular family names or historical events? Take note of all the details they find important to detail and how much attention, time, or other resources to emphasize them. Then, look at the local libraries. Is the main library for the County in your city or a neighboring one? When you go to the main one, study the local history that has been recorded there through periodicals. You can also check with the Historical 'Society. Find out who started your city and if your city represents a lot of 'firsts' for the city, your area, your state, etc. Ask what major events have happened in your city and what were their cause and effect. Find out how the city responded to these events, such as approve, up-rise, thrive, decline, etc. Other areas you can check would be the Chamber of Commerce educational institutions, research facilities, parks, cemeteries, streets named after people, museums, restored buildings, fire/police stations, and restaurants. When you examine restaurants, and churches, look for diversity, such as old verses new, ethnic, non-ethnic, specialty, locally owned, franchised, etc. Count how many hospitals, rehab centers, nursing homes, cancer treatment or Alzheimer units there. Consider whether or not they are medical teaching facilities. Visit the properties and talk to the people. Study police reports and statistics for this city. Look at logos on businesses or vehicles. Does the city seem family oriented? Look at the ways the neighborhoods are designed such as having sidewalks, or bike lanes, playgrounds, community clubhouses, close to schools, etc. Does your city have a natural division between other cities, or does it blend in? Is it a transportation hub?

SYNERGY OF THE AGES

Clearly this is a lot of information. It's not all intended to be done at once. Remember, there have already been people throughout the ages that have been diligent with their hands to the plow. For you to begin is to partner with the work done before you, alongside you, and for any work after you.

Begin to ask the Lord where to focus and He will point some things out to you. In time, you will have a better understanding of your cities Redemptive Design. When you begin your search, narrow down your choices to two or three. By reading this lesson, you will begin to eliminate those that obviously do not apply to your city. Hopefully, you will learn something about your territory that you didn't know before. All right! Let's get started.

Amos 1 and 2 lists the sins of different cities. All communities have most sins. There is nothing new under the sun. A demonic stronghold over a city will line up with the redemptive design of that territory. As you learned in IDENTITY, a stronghold can start as a wrong belief or bitter root judgment disguised as truth and enveloped in hopelessness to prevent operating fully in the Will of God. This stronghold will represent a perversion of the principle of each gift.

PROPHET / PERCIEVER

The Perciever's principle strength or weakness will line up with one's Design *or Purpose*. A Perceiver or Prophet City is known for their control. This design has a resistance to bondage or being told what to do. Even though they are verbally expressive and are able to articulate well, they have an opinion about everything. This city will communicate profoundly well. They believe that truth is truth and people should receive it. They administrate well because they can easily distinguish between right and wrong. They will also tend to resist hidden agendas and manipulation. This city is motivated by justice. They are also willing to stand alone if they believe in their cause.

Other characteristics of the Perceiver/Prophet City: Even though they themselves do not wish to be rescued, they will rescue everyone. Because this Design City is a hard-working city, they are the ones to build and restore an entire city, even a section or society within a city. They come along side and help with restoration initiatives and are capable of formulating new ideas. This Redemptive Design makes this city highly visible as excellent planners, and fiercely intentional. However, they are also known for interfering when not wanted or needed. They have a desire for excellence in all that they do. This will be reflected in their infrastructure and architecture.

Additionally, this type city is extrememly decisive. They will have a handle on the now but are focused on the future. They will have many research and development companies and new high-tech gadgets.

This design will demonstrate the largest range of emotions of any of others. They are passionate and intense. Some emotional

Kingdom Purpose

traits of the Perceiver/Prophet Redemptive City is the struggle with pride, bitterness and despair if or when things don't go the way they think. They will have a tendency to discriminate, yet are merciful toward the poor. They are fiercely competetive and independent. They have a passion to celebrate and are quick to find such an occasion. They demonstrate extreme emotions in most settings. They are extremely loyal and generous, but can be impulsive. They will take about six to eight seconds to make a deccision.

AUTHORITY: Over Poverty
STRONGHOLD: Fractured Relationships
INIQUITY: Normalization of Bitterness
VIRTUE: Be a Rebuilder
ROOT INIQUITY: Rights of Individuals

SERVANT

The principal strength or weakness of a Servant will line up with *Authority*. The outward social behaviors of this Redemptive Design will be reflective as a not being able to truly identify who they are. They are the brunt of endless jokes, living below the reality of who they really are. This City will carry a mantel of dishonor or invisibility for the community. In leadership, the representation will either be one of an exploitive predator type in nature or weak and enabling. When demonstrated in government, it causes real problems. There will be a lack in strong leadership and the need for strong leaders will be great. The land itself will draw predators and victims. There will be high volumes of murder, abuse, domestic violence, child molestation, addictions, homelessness, vagrancy, petty theft, and trafficking. There will likely be a strong death spirit on the land that leads to accidental deaths, violent deaths, and suicides. Abuse of anti-anxiety drugs will be prevalent in this territory due to stress and anxiety.

The Servant Design will prosper in agriculture and service industries. These sites do not hold much in way of things to do and see but are more of the 'drive-through' destinations. This territory is not offensive or disruptive, but sort of blend in. It tends to be the 'unwanted' or rural land, but they are easily exploited by leadership in churches, businesses, or home settings as the Servant Cities have difficulty saying no to competing demands around them. However, this also keeps them from having many enemies. If you find the Ruler City nearby, look for the Servant City. It will be shown by a predator victim relationship. This land is seen battling for legitimacy and self-worth. However, this Redemptive Design is a life-giver to those they serve and empower others to achieve. They are a platform for a second chance. They are able to identify the best in others even when no one else does. People with a Servant Redemptive Gift are typically drawn to these cities. Servants are blind to boundaries and do not defend their borders well. It is easy for them to be absorbed by more powerful cities because they do not make enemies and are included to be people pleasers.

To foster effectiveness through the authority of a Servant City, they will have to earn their authority. To whom much is given, much is required. The Servant will need to overcome evil with good in that city by restoring the walk of being like Christ. They can begin by blessing those places presently being occupied by curses. When the Servant City begins to speak the truth, it liberates the land while becoming life-givers to others. They demonstrate this by shepherding, nurturing, and empowering. Through intercession, leaders will need to focus on the curses of death by asking what defiled water, land, and atmosphere. Their decrees and declarations of restoration will break the curses of death.

AUTHORITY: Over the Land
STRONGHOLD: Victim spirit
INIQUITY: Denying One's God-Given Authority
VIRTUE: Walking in Dominion
ROOT INIQUITY: Peace at Any Cost

TEACHER

As a teacher in the Redemptive Design, the principal strength or weakness will line up with *Responsibility*. The Tribe associated with Teacher is Levi. Some of the behavioral tendencies of this Redemptive City will be a demonstration of a disproportionate number of Hospitals, whether teaching, specialty, rehabilitative, or nursing homes; medical doctors, research facilities, educational facilities, fine cuisine restaurants, parks, cemeteries, and churches than the population needs. You will also encounter a strong religious spirit due to the religious activity presiding in this territory. This will include many denominations, as well as cults, New Age, and overt occult practices. The same diversity is displayed through social and geographic or natural divisions. This religious spiritual influence will also place emphasis on its proud heritage through architecture and museums. Because they lean so much on the historical things, you will likely find a plethora of antique stores, historical homes, restored buildings, and numerous streets named after people. This city will be a city of prototypes; firsts, although they are slow in processing new ideas.

Reconciliation and restoration is part of this Design's birthright. Teacher Redemptive Cities set the standard and will make a way for reconciliation after there has been a violation of the standard. They will have a passive military presence and are considered a city of refuge. They tend to have a passivity in all sectors of society. Their leaders will make soft choices for convenience, control, or for relationships. Because the Teacher Design is considered a safe place of hospitality even for the wounded, there will be defilement of land and buildings.

The Teacher City flows in doctrine by establishing parameters while their strong sense of authority in the physical and spiritual moves people into the manifest presence of God through worship. This is a generational anointing. In order to foster strong moral virtues in a Teacher City, they will need to bring the true spirit-filled lifestyle of worship to God. They will need to build responsibility and integrity utilizing the follow through of practical tools like doing what they say they will do, showing up on time, ending on time, picking up trash, returning phone calls and emails, and taking personal responsibility.

AUTHORITY: Over Personal Responsibility
STRONGHOLD: Religious spirit
INIQUITY: False Worship, Idolatry
VIRTUE: Brings Sanctification & Worship
ROOT INIQUITY: Selective Responsibility

EXHORTER

This principal strength or weakness of the Exhorter will line up with *Reality of Sowing and Reaping*. The Exhorter Design is associated with the Tribe of Ephraim. The Exhorter Cities demonstrate an ability to be world-changers. These are the ones that also hold the religious history in their hands. They have an ability to orchestrate large gatherings. I would tend to believe that Bethel, NY would be considered an Exhorter City even though it was a rural city, it was known as a resort town that revolutionized an era that made it 'unforgettable' in our cultural history of music and arts. Bethel had a visionary occupant who could see a broader picture and saw how a larger number of people could be affected. Other examples may include Rome, or more accurately the Vatican City, Jerusalem, also known as the City of David, and London which is widely known as the financial hub of the world and Buckingham Palace. These types of cities are where empires are built because they have an expansionists component unseen elsewhere. Imagine what an Exhorter City can do with an Exhorter City territory and nation. It could set the stage for a worldwide movement. UNESCO's World Heritage is strongly protected in the Exhorted City of Amsterdam.

An Exhorter Design City will maintain a high-profile community through top notch advertising and promotion. They are relationally strong, even above doctrine and are masters of reconciliation. Unity is at the heart of an Exhorter. Unity is what drives them. This helps them to be Master of Communication, generally able to touch hearts in a broad manner. However, they have selective responsibility in being willing to confront others. They will refuse to risk relationships by confronting bad behaviors. They draw a melting pot of diversity. In an Exhorter City, horizontal relationships are the focus. They are extroverted, outgoing, and relational. Focus tends to be on self which drives the entertainment industry such as vacations, beaches, etc. They are centered on social affairs where the more the merrier and high society parties. They understand timing and realize that timing is everything.

An Exhorter City will exhibit major economic components especially in trade and commerce where retail is concerned. They will have more bureaucratic red tape to cut through while communicating in a tactful diplomatic way. They tend to be intensely busy, working long hard hours. Their business can be a weakness. They also tend to normalize sin and sensuality.

In order to foster virtue in the Exhorter City, they will need to call sin, 'sin' as they seek the glory of God and not those things that please them sensually. They must be willing to become holy. Their focus must be intentional about the willingness to experience rejection or discomfort in work and relationships. They will need to establish a high moral standard without compromise as they move toward a deeper walk in God while learning to steward time well.

AUTHORITY: Over Reality of Sowing & Reaping
STRONGHOLD: Worship of Pleasure
INIQUITY: Denial
VIRTUE: Embrace the Conflict
ROOT INIQUITY: Refusal to Risk Relationship

GIVER

The principal strength or weakness will align with *Stewardship*. The Giver City will be a platform to birth business, especially industries and ministries. Givers have a birthing anointing. They provide vital resources to those around them. Giver Design will have intense diversity through race, economy, denominations, and restaurants. They will have a tremendous focus on safety and security. The police and fire departments will be excellent. Because of this sense of security, they will lean toward being independent, either good or bad. They will not have the welfare mentality but are inclined toward a Religious spirit. The Giver City will have complex politics, will manage to hinder the birthing of new ideas. Focuses are centered around family, high-profile entertainment, parks, land trusts, conservation areas, showy governmental buildings, excellent school programs, as well as having a reputation for being a family vacation destination.

While the Giver City like to keep all of its options open, they have a keen sense of timing and have tremendous favor with money and resources. They are a catalyst for networking and understand there are resources seen and unseen. They cannot be manipulated in negotiations. They are called to come alongside the other six Redemptive Designs to help them birth, nurture and protect new ideas, projects, and strategies.

A Giver City abhors being needy and does not like to be vulnerable or needy. We need Christ. This independence from God opens a city up to 'turf wars and doors of control through the spirits of Leviathan and Jezebel. Through faith in Jesus Christ, *grace* is the undeserved gift of forgiveness. The gift is to return to dependency on God to become holy as He is holy. The virtue to foster in a Giver City is the restoration of dependency on God and not self, being vulnerable to allow Him to provide our safety and provisions. This breaks the spirit of fear and restores faith. This will break the Leviathan and Jezebel spirits. Gratefulness dis-empowers Leviathan. When faith is evident and the heart of thankfulness toward God is released from a Giver design, lies, deception, and control of Freemasonry is also broken. Evangelism will be birthed giving a faith-based model from which everyone can reap.

AUTHORITY: Over Stewardship
STRONGHOLD: Independence via Ownership
INIQUITY: Control

Kingdom Purpose

VIRTUE: Walking by Faith and Gratitude
ROOT INIQUITY: Fear

RULER/ADMINISTRATOR

The Ruler's principal strength or weakness will support *Freedom*. Behavioral characteristics of the Ruler Design will include endurance and resurgence. They are not just building a city, but an empire. Likewise, they are obsessive about expanding borders and will go to battle to do it. Typically, you see this as aggressive annexation and a political adeptness. The Ruler Design will demonstrate a healthy independence that doesn't look for outside consenting opinions. They do not explain or justify, they just do. They are vibrant, energetic, and busy. Usually the Ruler City will be the county seat or maybe even a state capital because they work with the existence of a centralized government and participate in all kinds of projects and accomplishments. Sometimes the results of a Ruler City will be disproportionate to the resources at hand.

A Ruler Redemptive Design will have a superiority complex with affinities toward the exploitation of the masses for gain. They will likely have a Predator spirit. Churches in the area will govern with control with a focus on mega churches with heavy-handed organizational structure. The atmosphere around the Ruler City is "Go, go, go."

When the Ruler City realizes it does not need to control others, it will begin to serve others. This is key to overcoming the curses introduced. Churches are not in place to control people, but to serve people and the communities they are in. As long as the community is life-giving, there is not the need to build an empire. When virtue is found, the community will see crime rates diminish.

AUTHORITY: Over Freedom
STRONGHOLD: Predator spirit
INIQUITY: Exploitation
VIRTUE: Being Life Giving
ROOT INIQUITY: Lawlessness & Covenant Breaking

Redemptive Purpose

MERCY/COMPASSION

Compassion's principal strength or weakness will embody *Fulfillment*. A Mercy is similar to Teacher City in that they are both cities of refuge, however the Mercy City will attract those who have been rejected by the broader culture because of their values. Mercy Design is known for their intolerance for intolerance. They have a tolerance for whatever goes. This makes them attractive to Predator & Victim spirits because of their kindness and willingness to accept injustice. In this city, you will have no issue finding the following characteristics: people pleasing, abusive leadership, hostile employers, mixtures in religion, indecisiveness to avoid hurt feelings, stuck in time warp, slow to make changes due to emotional processing, reluctance to embrace pain, heavy-handed and controlling politics, diverse populations, specialty shops, craft stores, little book retailers, safe and secure atmosphere, full of creativity through self-expression, immorality and sexual sins, and a broad cross section of world view, and cults such as Eastern Mysticism, New Age, Yoga, Voodoo, etc.

Due to the Victim spirits operating through this city, a significant amount of infirmity, financial devouring, physical abuse, sexual assault, and battered wife syndrome will abound in this territory.

This city will draw attraction for its Art Galleries, art classes, museums, street vendors that sell anything arts & crafts, and buildings with murals and painting inside or out.

When the virtues of a Redemptive Mercy City are restored, it will be a place of high worship with an open heaven. There will be no lines between the secular and the sacred because joy of life is the act of worship. An acceptance of the broken and rejected people will bring the power of God to heal and restore. People will be healed and liberated from the torment of infirmity in the presence of God. There will be a full expression of fulfillment within God's boundaries in the body, soul, and spirit, of the Mercy that will usher in the rebuilding of lives through faith in God. Mercy is the gift that Christ gives us through eternal life.

AUTHORITY: Over Fulfillment
INIQUITY: Pride in Denial
STRONGHOLD: False Fulfillment: Body, Soul, Spirit
VIRTUE: Pleasing God, Not Man
ROOT INIQUITY: Stubbornness

REVERSE THE CURSE

Change begins with prayer. Seek God's heart. Then begin to pray into the things He shows you by standing on His Word, declaring and decreeing, blessing the land and people, and worshipping God through the change. Secondly, be part of the solution. It is easy to stand and criticize, but if you do not become part of the solution, you will only become part of the problem. Research to ensure you get to the truth of what is at the heart of the situation. Find out if it is a governmental issue, funding issue, neighborhood issue, lack of education, or something else. Gather your facts, then find others who agree with you. Find out if this is a generational issue or if what you've identified was a temporary or new change. Develop a strategy while you continue to pray into the solutions.

Schedule meetings with key people. Get to the root of the stronghold. Address the fruit of the stronghold before going to loosen the stronghold. When you identify the stronghold, isolate it to give you the largest return. Make sure the City is ready for repentance when you go after the stronghold otherwise it could become seven times greater. Once you find the stronghold, keep looking until you find the root iniquity or sin.

THE WRONG INFLUENCE

The seven enemies of God are listed in the Book of Judges. Each one of these enemies of Israel was left by God according to Judges 3:4. *They were left to test the Israelites to see whether they would obey the Lord's commands, which he had given their ancestors through*

Redemptive Purpose

Moses. The Israelites lived among the Canaanites, Hittites, Amorites, Perizzites, Hivites, and Jebusites. They took daughters in marriage and gave their own daughters to their sons and served their gods.

When man does the opposite of what God desires, it causes spiritual strongholds. Territorial strongholds are the result of willful sins and sins of ignorance committed on the land repeatedly. Just as you read in Identity, that this opens doors to our souls, it also opens doors on the land. For instance, an addict goes through detox and finds success. He goes home everything is fine, and there are no issues. Five years later, his job moves him to a location where there is a predisposition to a stronghold of addictions on the land. Those familiar spirits begin to torment him and before long, he is caught right back into the whirlwind of addictions. Without complete deliverance from the spirit of addictions, a person can be led back into addictions by familiar spirits. They can be familiar spirits on a family member, a friend, an old lover, a house, a job, or the land.

I knew someone who had built a new house and had sold their home of thirty years to my husband and me. Before we actually moved into the old house, I had visited the couple in their new home. It felt clean and light. My husband and I felt very comfortable there.

When we moved into their old house, it felt like that couple still lived there. My husband and I went through and prayed over the house, anointing it. When we were done, it felt clean and peaceful. The heaviness had left. However, when we went back to the new house to visit the couple, what had left our house was now in theirs. We had bound the spirits and asked them to go, but they went to where they were accepted to be 'at home'. The couple never addressed the spirits because these were familiar spirits. Sometimes people do not want to be delivered from these spirits, because they feel like they will lose part of their identity. This is a lie! Those spirits prevent people from realizing their true identity. Evil spirits do not want people to become whole and healthy. It takes more work to accept things that are unfamiliar to us than it does for us to simply exists in the familiar.

Kingdom Purpose

It is important to understand, we do not blow into town and simply start going after spirits with guns blazing. This can get you in over your head. I've had people tell me. *Well, God just told me to go and pray.* I will ask them, *How much time did He give you to prepare to go pray?* If it is a simple prayer to repent for the sins on the land, fine. If it is a simple prayer to ask God to bless it, also fine. However, don't start praying down strongholds, or going after principalities and dominions unless you have:

1) Identified the root stronghold through the counsel of Holy Spirit and research.
2) Asked God for the strategy to know when, what, where and how to pray.
3) Spent time praying and fasting over this assignment.
4) Found your scriptures to stand on in reference to the assignment.
5) Have other intercessors praying protection over you, your family members (seed), the assignment (land), and your job or business (livelihood).
6) Have two or three like-minded people to take with you.

It is called doing your due diligence. I am not going to stop you from your assignment, but I will caution you if you head into battle without properly being prepared. David did not rush in to fight Goliath, no. He took time to pray. He gathered some artillery. He strategized with King Saul. Then, he went into battle. We all have PURPOSE and have purposes to fulfill in the earth. We need to have the wisdom Jesus demonstrated for us. What did Jesus do?

According to John 8:28, 12:50, and 14:31, Jesus did just as His Father told Him to do. He didn't add to or take away from what His Father said. We need to be obedient to God, but we also need to get the blueprints for how he wants us to do it. This kind of prayer goes into the legal realm of the enemy. He has been given the legal right to be there, so you have to close the door that gave him that initial legal right.

Matthew 15:13 says, *Every plant that my heavenly Father has not planted will be pulled up by the roots.* Jesus restored your authority through His mercy and grace. Now it is up to you to use it. God chooses us to do His work. It is not a request, but a command. Ephesians 4:28 says, *Let him who steals, steal no more. But rather, let him labor, performing with his own hands what is good, in order that he may have something to share with him who has need.* We need to go to work and pull up those roots that God has not planted. We learned to do this in our own lives by closing the door to sin in IDENTITY, now it is time to close the doors of iniquity on the land. Those roots of iniquity are choking out our blessings and the blessings of those in need. Some don't even realize that they are in need. When we begin to choke out the roots of iniquity in the land, people will be set free. The lost will see the need for Jesus in their lives.

BIRTHRIGHT REDEMPTION

In order to reverse the curse of a Redemptive Design City, we have to possess the birthright. The birthright is the one unique thing about that city that no other has. When you can properly identify the birthright, you will then be able to see God's objectives versus man's objectives. Find where someone believed a lie that led to wrong decisions reversing God's design, choking out the blessing and blocking the birthright. The birthright holds the key to unnlocking the curse.

Each of the seven enemies of Israel named in Judges 3 corresponds to one of the Redemptive gifts in Romans 12. Once you identify the Redemptive Gift or Design of a city, you can find its iniquity which introduces the curse. These seven enemies represent the strongholds and dominions that have been introduced through the souls of man's sins. The reason we spend time identifying these is to bring repentance so the curses on the land may be overcome, and the birthright of the land may be restored.

When praying for an individual or land to be delivered from a stronghold, the first step is *always*; **repent**. Whether it is for the sin, wrong emotion, believing the lie, unbelief, or whatever the case may be; begin with repentence. Next, *always* **forgive**. Remember, if we expect God to forgive, we too must be willing to forgive. We forgive those who committed the sin against us, someone else, or the land. We forgive those that had knowledge and did nothing, if applicable. Next, we bind the stronghold and command it to leave the person or territory. Then immediately ask Holy Spirit to fill the void of that stronghold with the remedy of that sin or emotion. The opposite is typically the antidote in God's Kingdom to kill and destroy the root. For instance, if murder is the stronghold, the antidote (antonym) is 'life' or 'preservation of life'. Lastly, we thank the Lord for His mercy and grace. Worship his endless love that continues to save us from ourselves and others. Strongholds are the perversion or opposite of God's design. When we break the strongholds, the fulfilling of our birthright will follow for us, others, and the land. When we are not walking in our birthright, we hinder our own personal development and the development of others around us. It literally brings a curse on what is meant to be our blessing. Malachi 2:1-4 really sums this up perfectly.

A land may have all seven curses because it will have on it what the previous people have left on it. When we discuss the land, consider these two things: the Cushan-rishathiam principle, and the Aram Naharaim principle.

The Cushan-rishathiam principle is when there is a generational doubling heritage of evil. Cushan means darkness, or a generational heritage of iniquity. Rishathaim means multiplying or the doubling of the iniquity. In history, look to see where there has been Druids, Shamans, Ancient Mayan kings, Freemasonry, or Anti-Christ spirit or acts of evil repeated through several generations. Look to the lands that are always in turmoil or war and have been for several decades or throughout history. These symptoms representat such places.

Aram-Naharaim means the land of two rivers. Just as there are two rivers of authority in every social institution or what we could even call the 'influential mountains'. This principle reflects a governmental river and a spiritual river. The government is to reflect the partnership in God, not to oppose Him or operate out of our own control. The spiritual river is for the purpose of bringing God's truth, knowledge, and revelation. Which govenment is vying for control? What spirit is behind the control?

Redemptive Purpose

We can be effective in our prayer lives when we are able to identify the need and know which direction to pray. Knowledge is half the battle. The rest is in our prayer discipline. We work within God's Times and Seasons to prepare battle on the land through prayer. We are not able to effectively live in our dominion without a sound prayer life. Overturning strongholds in the land begins in prayer as we also pray for the hearts of people to be changed. We research, identify, repent, forgive, bless, bind, break, loose, and decree victory in our land, the seven mountains of influence, and in the lives of the people. This is our PURPOSE.

9

*P*URPOSE WITHIN *P*URPOSE

Purpose is the reason for which something exists. A purpose is done or made regarding an intended result. We have discussed messianic purposes, physical purposes and ancestral purposes so far, but how does this relate to our purpose as individuals?

Without knowing your identity in Christ, pursuing your purpose is as useless as looking for a coin in the dark. Once you know who you are, the light comes on and you can see what you're after. Part of our purpose comes through our name, other parts through our gifts and callings, but all of our purpose reflects our Creator who had a specific plan for our lives before the foundations of the world. The word of God is the map to lead us to our purpose and identity.

But what if someone finds themselves walking outside of their purpose for a time? What if they made a poor choice or life simply got in the way? Are they cast out? No, an individual cannot change their purpose, but do determine its effectiveness. In rebellion from what God has purposed, by ignoring God's covenant, one disallows the miraculous wonders that are available through the covenant to aid and assist in a life fulfilled in purpose. What if they've missed God and moved off track from their purpose? Perhaps through procrastination or willful disobedience, someone has allowed oneself to miss out on God's perfect timing for their life, but through repentance, God will place them right where they are supposed to be. An individual's purpose doesn't ever leave them, but one can live an entire life without discovering it.

Although our purpose in life does not change, our priorities in a specific season certainly do. My focused intention changed the moment my father was diagnosed as being in the fourth year of a five-year disease. My weekends were suddenly consumed with traveling eight hours to spend time with my father and relieve my mother of nursing duties, while also assisting my daughter with SAT preparation, graduation details, and college interviews on the home front. Those family matters became high priorities over the regular obligations in business and personal affairs.

DISTRACTIONS HINDER PURPOSE

When we encounter challenges, we modify our behavior to better face them, but that does not change our purpose, it simply redirects our focus. However, sometimes we allow distractions to take us off course from our intended purpose. This is when the enemy gets a foothold into our lives and trouble typically follows. We can avoid this by remaining in tune with the voice of the Lord so that we see and hear accurately. If the cloud isn't moving, stay put. If the fire by night is moving, it's time to go. Your God-established purpose doesn't change, but your function in it may according to the time and season you're in or your response to God's leading.

Any hinderances from realizing, actualizing, and demonstrating our purpose is a distraction. Distractions will come in all forms but are typically associated to unhealthy boundaries through relationships utilizing the Drama Triangle. Distractions come in the form of work, desires, ambition, greed, cultural influence, family, friends, religion, politics, striving, competition, poverty, sickness, lawlessness, slothfulness, and gluttony. The kingdom of darkness will use any hinderance it can, typically things that are already in your life, to take your focus off your relationship with God in order to deter your fulfillment of purpose. Healthy boundaries and having a clear understanding of balancing life's responsibilities according to God's ways is a foundational key for intentionally fulfilling your purpose.

REALIGNING WITH OUR PURPOSE

As believers, we can make choices that interrupt our growth in our purpose. Inner healing and deliverance allows us to identify where those roadblocks exist so that we can break them up and pave a solid foundation through forgiveness, repentance, and renunciation. We can realign with God's spoken destiny over our lives through simple prayers. That's all it takes! And that's all it took for me.

I suffered from self-image issues almost two decades ago. How could I be strong and do what I was called to do when I saw myself as worthless? My identity perception flaws needed to be dealt with in order to build the platform I could stand upon in order to walk into the fullness of my purpose. When I realized this, I knew what I needed to do. I became my best student. I worked through my own inner healing and deliverance, and through that time, the Lord prompted me to go deeper in my relationship with him. I am a remarkably different woman than I was in 1999. I have realigned with my purpose.

Through my realignment, my ability to train others expanded. As one who has received so much deliverance, I understand the freedom it can offer. My heart desires to see others recognize their true identity and see themselves the way the Father sees them—beautifully and wonderfully made. I don't have to live for the approval of others anymore. I'm running after the approval of my Papa-God, and that's all I need.

Once you walk in the truth of who you are, rejection can no longer define you because you live conscious of your Father's unconditional love. Your faith may be tested, but rejection belongs under your feet. The trigger empowers the choice to take that thing that wants to be our stronghold and put it under our feet. By choosing righteously, it becomes a platform for us to walk in our purposes in a deeper anointing, and deeper calling. Deep calls unto deep.

Sadly, many believe they are beyond the need for inner healing or deliverance. Unknowingly they create havoc all over the body of Christ. Many of my battle wounds have been inflicted by other believers who don't deal with their demons; literally. If you ever want to know if you have something that needs to be dealt with, just ask someone who knows you well enough to tell you the truth. Contrary to popular belief, you are probably the last to realize it.

THE POWER OF AGREEMENT

God created man for relationship. He gave us free will because he wanted us to choose life. Creation was his choice. But our choices also have consequences that affect the people in our sphere of influence, even when we don't see it.

Through the law of entanglement, whatever is loosed in heaven, is loosed on earth, and whatever is bound on earth, is bound in heaven. Therefore, if we pray and come into agreement for something, we are releasing it in the earth. We need to understand that we have the authority to decree a thing that is not as though it was. We have the power to establish the will of God in the earth.

But what if we decree a thing that's not God's will? The Tower of Babel was built by people in perfect agreement functioning with a focused intention while worshiping false gods. God himself said that because they are one, there is nothing that can stop them, and his response was to divide their tongues. They could no longer accomplish a thing because they were unable to communicate. Yep, God will do things like that.

If we speak in the tongues of the Holy Spirit, and we unite under the power of agreement, there is nothing that can stand in our way. That is why we discussed the Seven Mountains of Babylon—where the Tower of Babel was built. The men who built the tower wanted to be like God, but they were operating out of the wrong side of their gifts, and they brought curses on the land through their defilement. Imagine if they had repented, turned from their wicked ways and lived on the righteous side of their giftings. Imagine what kind of godly government could have been made. Imagine what could happen if the body of Christ worked together to accomplish God's heart for earth.

REDEMPTIVE HEALING

Why did Noah have to build an ark? God said he was going to send the rain to redeem the land from its sin by starting over, but the Lord wanted to preserve Noah. He was a righteous man, so he had him build an ark out of gopher wood and you know the rest of the story.

But the water itself was only judgement; it couldn't purify the earth. There had to be repentance for the depravity of man, and prayer to restore the earth free of past sin, blessed and redeemed. We don't read about that in Genesis, but we know it happened because of the Lord's covenant with Abraham. But what if Noah had not cleansed the world through prayer? Those who planted the seeds of wickedness would be gone, but the seeds they imparted would remain in the earth. Without prayer, it is impossible to experience redemptive healing.

Jesus did nothing outside of his father's will. He was sinless. When Jesus came, he healed the sick, cast out devils and signs and wonders followed him. He delivered the people from the power of the enemy. Similarly, redemptive healing is like deliverance healing for the land. When we pray over the land and operate in our redemptive giftings, the atmosphere shifts and healing is manifested.

But we must be careful to function properly in our redemptive gifts so that we do not invoke the curses on ourselves, our families, ministries and jobs. Why? Because of the law of entanglement. If God gives me a business, I am the owner of that enterprise, and therefore, the business takes on an identity through me. So if I'm operating under a curse, that curse will percolate through my business. That doesn't necessarily mean my business will go bankrupt, but it may translate into the way I treat my employees or manage my finances. It may cause me to exploit others in and around my business. Living in the curse of an unredeemed land can affect any area of your life, that's why we must pray for restoration and walk in our proper giftings.

I've witnessed families in business together. Traits, attitudes, practices, and other things from the family trickle down into the business of that family, for better or for worse. This is because of those same laws of entanglement. A person's conduct affects those around them. This law does not apply exclusively to business. It could be associated to marriage, finance, education, government, and more.

When we restore our redemptive gifts through repentance, we minimize the downfalls we experience in our lives. I am not exempt from that number. I have to work to keep my fleshly tendencies under foot, especially when my weaknesses rise up within me. They present the perfect opportunity to restore order in my life through repentance. This is why we can go into the Babylonian realms of influence and stand confidently, knowing who we are and what to do. When we're operating in alignment with our redemptive gifts, it affects the land we walk on.

Crispin always says, *I don't let their actions change my actions. I am going to continue to do what I know is right. They can do whatever they want. I hold myself accountable.* We ask, Is that integrity? Integrity is choosing to do the right thing even when no one is watching.

REPENTANCE

We've seen that before healing can come to a land, prayer has to go forth, but what about repentance? That 180° turn is an element in redemptive healing that we often overlook.

During the National Day of Prayer, I was privileged to read our mayor's speech ahead of time. It was a beautiful declaration, precise and well written. But as I read it, I couldn't help but wonder, *Where's the repentance?*

Even as believers, we tend to get caught in a vicious cycle of self-focus. We pray for the Lord's blessing, but we're not willing to confess our failures, acknowledge our imperfection, and ask for forgiveness. Repentance requires a desire for change. It's not simply saying you're sorry, it's declaring that you want to live your life differently, that you don't want sin to be your identity and you want his spirit to cleanse and renew you. All the prayer and anointing in the world will not place you above the need for repentance.

Kingdom Purpose

This same principle applies to inner healing ministry. When I'm praying with someone for emotional healing or deliverance, I always make repentance the first step and follow it with forgiveness. The people I counsel will often say things like, *What does forgiveness have to do with my healing? When we confess our sins, he is faithful and just to forgive, right?* There is an important distinction to be made here. Where our sin is concerned, yes, repentance enables forgiveness, but Scripture says that God cannot forgive us until we forgive others. So even though we repent of our wicked ways, we're still missing half the point if we don't forgive those who have trespassed against us.

Repentance for ourselves is not sufficient because we are affected by the sins committed against us through the law of entanglement. Therefore, when we forgive others for setting obstacles in our way, it's sweet incense to the Lord. It's selflessness. You're not only looking out for yourself through repentance, but you're looking out for your brothers and your sisters as well; you have become your brother's keeper. You're now showing that Christ-like love that cannot be earned and you're walking in total freedom.

Grace is a gift we receive, that is not earned. We haven't done anything to earn it, not one iota. When we extend that grace to others, it brings the sweetness of the Lord. He is delighted and says, *Now, I'm going to show you so much mercy. I'm going to show you so much grace.* Now you've demonstrated grace through forgiveness in the things that are undeserved the same way God has shown you grace.

Grace moves the heart of God, and it brings a compassion even when we really don't deserve it. We really deserve judgment; we really deserve to lose a year of growth because we've been walking out disobedience; we've been hearing the voice of the Lord, yet we're continuing to do our own independent thing. Grace is a splendid gift. We shouldn't take it for granted. When we pair repentance with forgiveness, it allows God's grace to come and abound.

Purpose within Purpose

Repentance and forgiveness appeals to the nostrils of God like meat stacked on the barbeque. He loves the aroma of grace and mercy being demonstrated by his children. He sees that they are following after his footsteps. It makes him well up inside. Moreover, where his grace abounds, cleansing and purifying transpires for the one forgiving and the one who needed to be forgiven. It creates a seed bed for the individual who had done wrong to come to their own place of repentance. Is it through our prayers? Yes. Does that mean that they had the full gift of repentance? No, not until they repent for themself, but it releases them from the judgment held over them. This makes room for Holy Spirit conviction to turn their hearts because they're experiencing grace that they have not experienced before. If they will act upon their conviction and repent, their lives can be transformed. This is the power of prayer.

We have the power of spiritual influence for forgiveness. The person we pray for could have 10,000 lives attached to them, lives that are influenced through that prayer of forgiveness. That's the power of God's transformation; his multiplication is exponential, so much larger than we can think or imagine because what influences one person continues through generations. It may just look like an individual to us, but see their seed brings a harvest. Forgiveness brings a harvest that we do not yet know, but God does. He knows the sand in the sea; he knows the hairs on our heads; he knows the number of stars in the sky. He knows and keeps count of the number of seed affected by one prayer of forgiveness. This is the transformation one person's prayer can make.

We are to pray prayers of repentance and prayers of forgiveness. Then we bind and break. We bind up the evil spirits. We break the curses off because we have the authority. God has done his piece to bring the grace. Once grace has been applied, it breaks the power of the curse. Hence, we can bind and break those curses from here on out. We can release heaven on earth, escorting the kingdom of heaven here and coming into agreement with him from earth into heaven.

Finally, we fill the place of repentance with glory, peace and spirit rain. We fill it with the presence of God. We don't leave that land void. If I dig a hole for seed and I leave it empty, it's still just a hole. However when I fill it up with something new, it can produce something. The goal is to produce the opposite fruit of what it was bearing, the sinful nature, before grace. If there was fear, we bring peace. If there was an anxiety, we bring grace. If there was inflammation, we bring healing. Whatever the opposite is, we bring it to wherever we have influence or wherever there is the need. Whatever we pray and establish through restoration should reflect God's original intent.

This is what Jesus did. Then he gave us the Comforter to fill us and instruct us on how to pray. When we don't know how to pray, we pray in tongues until we get the answer on how to pray. He gives us the strategies to know what is needed. He tells us this is what the land is yielding, we can witness the fruit. If the root of that fruit is fear, we first deal with the fruit. It could be a spirit of anxiety, stress, fear of death, dread, depression, panic attacks, etc. Just pluck it, bind it, and chunk it. Now all that rotten fruit doesn't weigh the tree down anymore. It makes the tree lighter so you can pull up all the roots. Evil spirits entangled themselves with other evil spirits to give themselves power, so listen to Holy Spirit to see if there are any other spirits attached. We don't stop there. No. Let's get the roots. We bind them, cut them up, and burn them up. In the natural, you bind the demon of 'Fear', renounce any agreements made with the spirits of fear, break its power of influence over the person, land, business, etc. and command it to go to the feet of Jesus for its directives. Next, we ask for the spirit of peace to come and fill up the place where the root of fear once occupied. We bless the spirit of peace to flourish and grow.

When you have a person that has a wound, the enemy will come and infect that wound over and over again. Every time that person encounters fear, it brings another spirit of fear or anxiety, and it just keeps adding and adding until you think that person can never get free of fear. But it can be done. You eliminate those fruits until you can get to that first one. When they are all gone, you pray the blessing. THIS IS IMPORTANT- Fill that empty spot, plant a seed with one of the Fruits of the Spirit. We do not leave the voided spot empty, or the enemy will find it as a clean house and re-enter. Therefore, we ask father to place one of His fruits of the Spirit that is opposite to what the enemy planted. Righteous fruit replaces unholy fruit and evil is overturned.

When we talk about going into the mountains, just your presence brings an atmospheric shift to that mountain. It is through your identity that you bring an impartation of what is needed in that mountain because you are there in this appointed time or season. Your sound is a vital piece to the recovery of that mountain toward righteousness and yet, we don't even have to utter a sound. Spiritually, the blood of Jesus in us merges with our DNA which creates sound that is released as we are being intentional in our purpose.

Your body has this DNA code that is a musical soul. Your blood is moving through your body. Close your ears and listen for the blood moving through your body. Isn't that amazing? Sound and light are the same they just move differently through what is referred to as waves. The distinction is made through their speed. When I hit a musical note on a keyboard, it is reflected as a color. There are certain mathematicians that see numbers as color. They don't actually see the numbers like we do, so when they hear a musical note, they see that number and they see that color. Isn't that just phenomenal? When your musical DNA is resonating, it creates a color. Each individual has a sound and light identity. When you are filled with Holy Spirit, your sound and light is merged with his. It becomes a symphony of both light and sound and it makes up your DNA song.

If there is one thing that I want you to take away from this book, it's that you would know that regardless of your situation, background, or perception of yourself, you were created with purpose. This book has been an exploration of how you are to operate with your purpose and how God can use you to advance his kingdom. However, never become so wrapped up in the work that you overlook that you live because God desires a relationship with you. You have purpose in his love. You were made for loving him, and he made you because he had more love than he knew what to do with. We can talk about different types of purposes, how to use them, how to change atmospheres and take back mountains, but if you do all of that without knowing that God's purpose is to show his love to you and the world, then you miss the whole point.

Our identity shows us who we are in Christ, our purpose tells us why we were made, and our authority is God's word on the earth exercised through us. Do not get so caught up in the details that you miss the simplicity of the gospel. Jesus summarized it well in Matthew 28. *All authority has been given to me in heaven and on earth. Go therefore and make disciples of all the nations, baptizing them in the name of the Father, the Son and the Holy Spirit.* We're here to spread his name across the world and to tell an orphaned people what their Father honestly thinks about them. If your life message preaches anything short of that, you're preaching the wrong gospel.

I commission you the same way Jesus did his disciples: Go! The time is now. The Kingdom is at hand. You are a child of God, filled with his Spirit, consumed by his love, and carrying his authority. You want for nothing, and you have nothing to fear. For every purpose God has appointed to you, he has equipped you. He desires that we live in peace with one another, fulfilled through the seed, land and livelihood provided by covenant and birthright. These are his kingdom principles.

Let's live purposefully together, as one body, one people under our God to see his kingdom come, his will be done.

Rebecca Bennett and her husband, Crispin, are the founders of Wells of SouthGate, based in Mississippi. Their vision includes an apostolic hub across the Gulf Coast for the training and equipping of the ecclesia in this new era: "Out of Error," where operating in the fivefold gifts is not only taught but demonstrated and discipled. Through the School of Ministry, believers become more effective within every sphere of influence.

Rebecca's passion is to show people how to live in the fulness of all life has to offer. Wells of SouthGate has a community-minded focus for basic life skills, education, leadership training, job placement, business planning, home-buying strategies, and finance. It presently partners with several ministries and is affiliated with Network Ecclesia International (NEI).

Since her teens, Rebecca has honed skills as an entrepreneur. Today, her businesses operate in the Kingdom Principles and core values that Rebecca teaches in this series. Because of their success, she can spend more time teaching others.

It was late September in 2017, when a download of thoughts came funneling through Rebecca's mind. As she jotted them down, they became separated into four sections. After a few weeks of contemplation, they became Identity, Purpose, Authority and Leadership, what is now *The Destiny Series*. It is a journey of education, experience, and hope; one that she longs to take you on, to the glory of God.

For scheduling speaking and teaching engagements with Rebecca, visit any of her websites:

www.rebeccadbennett.com

or

www.kligulfcoast.com   www.wellsofsouthgate.com

The Destiny Series Books

STRATEGIC TRAINING TO DISCOVER YOU

The Destiny Series is designed to help you discover the who and the why that you are. You are designed to become a great leader that God intended you to be, and you can reach your maximum potential in the ministry that the Lord Jesus gave every person (Matthew 28:19).

This dynamic and interactive series is available for individual or group study, as well as an author led course. To learn more, visit **www.rebeccadbennett.com** or **www.kligulfcoast.org**.

A Publishing Assist Company
Honor & Excellence as the seedbed of your written work

3Trees Publishing was born the result of the architectural build out of Wells of SouthGate. Following the blueprints for the region, 3Trees Publishing serves to reconnect creatives with their kingdom calling by supplying a framework of excellence for all printed work. This endeavor reintroduces and reconstitutes the original intent and design for the Spanish West Florida Territory and beyond. Let the expression of your purpose be revealed as you prepare legacy for those who come after. For more information, contact us at **3treespublishing@gmail.com**.

THE NAME Speaks by Angela Broussard
His sound reverberates. Can you hear Him speak your name?

It is said that life is a journey and we are pilgrims on it. Discovering our strengths, weaknesses and opponents on the journey exposes the reality of the spiritual realm - and just how fortified it is. Each installment of Doors, Gates, and Thresholds will equip you to successfully navigate the unseen structural components of both the Kingdom of God and the Kingdom of darkness, leading you to victory upon victory. This, in turn, will empower the corporate expression of the Ekklesia, releasing power in greater measure, and you bring your victory to bear upon the whole.

The Name Speaks is the introduction to the Master Poet and His creation: you. Engage in the formation of your identity within the large context of the Kingdom, and come to know your vital role in service to the King. For more information visit: www.silvercornerstone.com or www.kligulfcoast.org.

Designs x Laura
Let's manifest your vision

Designs x Laura is a brand and service for helping others find and interpret their vision. Whether you offer a product or service, are new or established in your field or maybe don't know what the next step is for you, you're covered!

For web design, graphic design and marketing services, please visit www.designsxlaura.com or email contact@designsxlaura.com for a free consultation. If you don't see a specific need listed, feel free to reach out and our team will be happy to assist and discuss the innovation of your ideas.

Education

MAKING EXCELLENCE VISIBLE

KLI GULF COAST

The leadership institute of choice prepares you for leadership in the Kingdom of God. The strategy of KLI Gulf Coast is individualized. Your leadership training can begin at any level of spiritual and ministry maturity. We start where you are with what you do. As one can function in any aspect of culture, once taught to function in kingdom culture, the Institute educates and prepares students for any arena of occupation. We honor kingdom leaders from every walk of life. Students come from many professions and occupations.

Partnered with KLI Jacksonville, our course intensives develop mature individuals to impact the current culture with Kingdom culture. Determine today to engage your life's work at the starting gate of Kingdom Leadership Institute Gulf Coast. For more information, or to enroll, visit www.kligulfcoast.org or contact us at kligulfcoast@gmail.com.

We Bring The Trainer To You.

Call today to discuss and implement the strategic training that's best for your business or field of influence!

838 Howard Ave
Biloxi, MS 39532

228-331-0017

www.wellsofsouthgate.com

Wells of SouthGate is a training, equipping, and activating center on the Mississippi Gulf Coast. Our passion is to see each person matured to fulfill our God-given dreams and destiny, to become a flourishing, contributing member of their society. For more information, visit our website: **www.wellsofsouthgate.com**.

www.ingramcontent.com/pod-product-compliance
Lightning Source LLC
Chambersburg PA
CBHW050250120526
44590CB00016B/2297